Dirty Thirty

A Memoir

Asa Akira

CLEiS
PRESS

Published in the United States by Cleis Press, an imprint of Start Midnight, LLC, 101 Hudson Street, Thirty-Seventh Floor, Suite 3705, Jersey City, NJ 07302.

Printed in the United States.
Cover design: Scott Idleman/Blink
Cover Art: David Choe
Text design: Frank Wiedemann

First Edition.
10 9 8 7 6 5 4 3 2 1

Trade paper ISBN: 978-1-62778-164-0
E-book ISBN: 978-1-62778-165-7

Dedicated to Toni

Intro

It was one month and thirteen days before my birthday. I wasn't normally one for counting down to holidays—especially when they were personal—but this was a special one, my thirtieth. So far, anticipating it was turning out to be a lot like waiting for a tab of acid to hit; one by one, as my peers experienced the customary thirty-year-old freak-out, I patiently waited for my turn. With every moody period day, I wondered: Is this is it—am I feeling it? Is this the beginning stage? Is this when I start to panic about my age? I think I'm feeling it! But as every period ended, I realized no, this was not it. I was still stone-cold sober.

For as long as I could remember, I'd known with absolute certainty that turning thirty came with a whole show of dramatics. Knowing this was like knowing the earth is round. On television, in the movies, there was always the girl on her birthday, crying because nothing had gone according to plan, crying because her boyfriend had not proposed, crying because of, well, just the overall pressure of being a real-life adult. It had been ingrained in me, the idea of the thirty-year-old's panic attack. Whenever someone asked me my age, I found myself automatically saying something like "I can't believe I'm about to be thirty. That's *so* crazy."

The truth was, it didn't feel crazy at all. I almost—no, absolutely—wished it did. It was what I'd been expecting. Sometimes I would try to force myself to think of all the things I thought I'd have by this age but didn't: a child, a primary care physician, a credit card. I'd close my eyes and concentrate on thoughts like: My mom was already pregnant with me at this age. Biggie had already been dead for seven years when his thirtieth birthday came around. I didn't think I'd be thirty with Hello Kitty stickers still on my phone. I didn't think I'd be thirty and still be watching *Teen Mom*; grownups didn't do that! And certainly, I didn't think I'd be thirty and still be using the word "grownup."

That weekend, we were in Philly: Me, Jay, Mike. They were brothers, guys I had known since I was nineteen years old. I met them when I was waitressing at an underground poker club in New York City—these guys had known me since my boobs were real. Since before I had worked in the adult industry, in any capacity. Since I had still lived at home with my parents. Since before I was married, the first time. Now, whenever I had a feature-dance gig on the East Coast, I had them drive up from New York City to help me. It's not a glamorous job, helping me on the road—it's all staying in cheap hotels, counting dirty singles, making sure I don't get raped during lap dances. It's a job that pays alright, but it's not like they needed the money. I like to tell myself they're in it more for the intangible compensation of their old friend's company.

We were sitting around the table in my dressing room. *Dressing room*. A term I'd come to use very lightly. It's rare that a strip club has an official room solely dedicated to housing the feature performer. There were no "green rooms" in the feature dancing world. One time, a club just put me in a spare bathroom; I sat on the toilet to strap my heels on before going onstage. Tonight, we were lucky: They had given us a nice "champagne" room to use. *Nice.* Another word I'd come to use lightly. If you ever get the chance to go into a champagne room with the lights on, I strongly suggest you don't take it. It will make you question why a place like a strip club would decide on fabric upholstery.

The guys were counting the singles I had just made onstage, while I looked at my phone while wearing nothing but a towel, my feet crossed on the table. We probably looked like a scene out of some gangster movie, only with much smaller denominations of money. I scrolled through my Twitter feed.

"Oh shit!" I sat up, stomping my six-inch heels on the floor. "The AVN nominations are up."

I scanned through the list looking for my name. I found it a few times: best anal scene, best solo scene, best website...

I couldn't fucking believe it. Squinting my eyes, I looked at the list again—maybe I had missed something—using my finger, pointing at each name, making sure it was not mine. I did this four times before giving up.

For the first time in five years, I was not nominated for performer of the year.

I looked up to see that the guys were finished counting the singles.

"Well? How'd you do?" Jay asked.

"I'm up for a bunch," I casually answered, not wanting to seem like I cared. "Except for performer. It's fine though, I mean I already won it two years ago—plus, it's not fair if a contract star gets nominated for it anyway. The other girls work way more. Like, I really don't care," I said way too fast.

"Cool," Mike answered. The guys knew me well enough to know that I was lying. That I did care. That I felt like shit. They also knew me well enough to know that discussing it would only make it worse. Pretending he needed to go do something, Mike left the room. Jay soon followed, mumbling that he was thirsty. Silently, I thanked them—I was sure my pride could not have continued the conversation further.

I didn't always care about the awards. My third year into porn, my date to AVN was the original Gonzo Queen herself, Jenna Haze. As we got our makeup done for the show in her hotel room, I distinctly remember being shocked at how nervous she seemed, unable to sit still in the chair—she was Jenna Haze, a huge star by then, winner of dozens of awards, one of the biggest names in porn ever.

"I'm so nervous!" Jenna had squealed, gripping the armrests on the makeup chair. "I just want to win one. Once I win one, I'll be fine."

Did she know these were just porn awards? Winning an award in porn, wasn't that like being the tallest midget? Did it really matter so much? Without saying anything, I silently judged her as she lost cool points in my mind. It's that classic thing about meeting your idols: They become real human beings, with real insecurities and personality flaws.

That night, I won my first award. It was for best double penetration scene, which had been my first DP, ever. And then I won for best anal. And then best lesbian three-way. I won five awards total that night.

And I came to understand Jenna's love of winning.

The next year, I was the same nervous wreck Jenna had been. I even repeated the exact phrase I had found so ridiculous twelve months ago: "I just want to win one. Once I win one, I'll be fine." I had tasted the fruit, I wanted more. Only, rather than fruit, it was more like an illegal controlled substance—I *craved* more. I was genuinely crushed when I didn't win performer of the year, despite winning seven other awards that night, the most of any performer.

Finally winning performer of the year the year after that was one of the best moments of my life, but it followed a nervous breakdown in my hotel room while waiting for the show to start. And the year after that, when I won a mere total of one award, my only consolation was the two cheeseburgers I ate alone, in silence, in my hotel room after the show.

When Jay and Mike came back to the dressing/"champagne" room in time for my next stage show, I was still sitting in the same spot, chain-smoking. They were kind enough to not mention anything, only ordering me to get dressed to go onstage.

The rest of the night, I was on autopilot. I went on stage, shook my ass, met fans, gave lapdances, didn't get raped (thanks Jay and Mike!), and went back to the hotel.

I texted Dee after I got out of the shower.

How much longer do you think I can be in porn?

She wrote back immediately: *Are you asking 'cause we are now 30?*

Holy shit. I realized that, like everything else in my life, my version of the thirty-year-old panic attack was the porno version. Was it over for me? Was I officially a MILF now? Were people no longer interested in seeing my gaping asshole?

What if my problem wasn't that I wasn't peaking yet—what if my problem was that I had peaked *too soon*?

It got me to thinking that, if anything, I felt I'd done *too much* to be only thirty. I'd had two abortions, which was just about the most shameful thing in my life. One was perfectly excusable, every girl is entitled to it—mistakes happen, and you learn from them. But two? Come on, get your shit together, stop telling so many guys to cum in you. I'd been to jail, survived a minor opiate addiction. I'd contracted countless STDs, had more boyfriends than Lindsay Lohan, and fucked so many guys that my body count was an (extremely rough) estimate. I'd been married in Vegas (twice)! I'd been divorced once. I'd stripped, shot porn, worked in a dungeon, even hooked a couple of times. Worst of all, I'd smoked cigarettes for over ten years, and even though I said I'd quit, I was still smoking when at parties, on vacation, on set, and pretty much just around people in general. On paper, I was Patty and Selma from the—At least fifty years old, and that was being nice.

With one question, Dee had given me the best birthday gift: my customary thirty-year-old freak-out.

Haiku

Still in bed at noon
Everyday is Saturday
When you are a whore

First Encounters

I was flying home from a dance gig with my friend Bill. I call him my friend because "assistant" sounds pretentious, "roadie" sounds like I think I'm a rockstar, and "bodyguard" is ridiculous, considering he is a five-foot-three, fifty-four-year-old Chinese man (not the *Kung Fu* kind) in thick glasses who gets his nails painted when he comes with me for a pedicure. Also, he jerks off while wearing women's underwear. I suppose I also call him my friend because he is. Our unlikely friendship started when I was looking around for a driver. Not that I don't drive, but as the stereotype goes, I don't drive well.

"Oh, I got the perfect person for you," my friend Dave replied when I asked him if he knew of anyone. Dave and I co-host a biweekly podcast in which we attempt to abstain from talking about anal sex, and fail every time. This is not a running gag, but a real-life objective. "His name's Bill, he drives hookers."

"Are you calling me a hooker?"

"No, of course not."

"Whatever. I kind of am."

When Bill came to pick me up on his first day on the job, Dave had given him strict orders not to speak to me. It was a joke, but the kind that was half-true: I hate making pointless small talk. Yet, when I got into his car, something about his smile just invited me in.

"Hi, I'm Bill."

That was all he said to me. He warmly introduced himself to my husband Toni, who had walked me out to the car in case my new driver turned out to be a weirdo rapist, but after that, Bill was silent. Silent, but not unfriendly. Something about him interested me—this man drove hookers? He was in his fifties, yet he was dressed like a teenager. I could see under the steering wheel that he wore shiny black leggings under his basketball shorts. His pinky nail was half an inch longer than the rest of his nails. With his plump face, faux Mohawk hairdo, and thick-rimmed glasses, he looked like a Chinese Chicken Little.

"So you drive hookers?" I finally broke the silence after five minutes. What continued was an hour-long conversation on hookers versus escorts. Where escorts saw one client once in a while for a thousand dollars-plus, hookers saw as many as ten clients a day for as low as one hundred bucks per guy. They often did "in-calls," where they rented out a motel room, churning the johns in and out all day long. As was always the case when hookers were mentioned, I was highly interested, and naturally, we hit it off.

I used Bill as a driver when I needed one, and sometimes even when I didn't. He became something like a friend whom I paid. He came with me to events, appearances, sets, interviews, and hung out with me like any two people in a platonic relationship. When it came time for my next feature-dance gig, I asked him if he'd like to come and roadie for me. I told him his job was to carry my suitcases, collect the dollar bills off the stage after I danced, and help me sell merchandise at the end of the night. Being a fairly easy job, which paid well for the amount of work, Bill was up for it.

The gig went well, and we had just boarded our flight back home to LA. As Bill put our things in the overhead bin, I sat in my window seat and checked my Twitter. Scrolling as fast as I could through tweets and retweets of photos of my anus that people had posted, something caught my eye:

You're on my flight.

I looked up and around, but didn't see anyone looking at me. I clicked on the profile, and it was a man named Keith. His profile photo was of a man in a grey hoodie—immediately, I realized I had passed him on my way to my seat. He was sitting down in an aisle seat, in the very same hoodie as his profile picture. I noticed him because he was handsome with stubble, and well, as anyone who knows me is aware, I'm a sucker for a man in a grey hoodie. I wrote him back.

Hi :)

I scanned through his profile. He seemed to have a big following, especially for a guy. What did he do? I went to his photos. He was in a wheelchair. *Maybe he's injured and in a wheelchair temporarily,* I thought. I looked at the date—it was posted only a day earlier. I quickly looked through the rest of his photos, and realized this wheelchair thing was permanent. I looked back at my own profile. He had written me again.

I'm a big fan. Follow me so I can DM you.

I did as he said and sent him a private message.

Hey! Following u now :)

I went back to his profile as I waited for a reply. Yes, he was definitely full-time in a wheelchair—it seemed a good portion of his tweets were promoting events for the handicapped. I wondered what kind of wheelchair guy he was—Paraplegic? Quadriplegic? Munchausen? He wrote back.

Come sit next to me.

I was surprised at how direct he was. I looked next to me at Bill, who was engrossed in the free issue of *SkyMall*, reading it with his glasses in his hand, the magazine inches away from his face.

Sorry, can't - I'm sitting with my friend.

Honestly, I was glad to have an excuse to stay in my seat. I was intrigued by this hot wheelchair man, sure, but what would I do sitting next to him on a four-hour flight? It was too much time next to a stranger, however good-looking he was. Just then, the flight attendant's voice came on, making the announcement it was time to shut our electrical devices off. I almost did just that, when I noticed I had another message from him.

Tell your friend he can switch seats with my friend for a bit.

I was amazed at how much he was pushing for this, and I think I liked it. But like I said, I hate small talk, and four hours was just too long for awkward conversation.

I'll come say hi when we land, shutting off.

I quickly typed, and put my phone away.

Social media has been around as long as I've been in porn. I can't imagine the business without it—when I shot my first scene, Myspace was still big, and I still remember fighting with my ex-boyfriend about putting him in my top eight.

"No one wants to see that," I would tell him, as I chose eight of my friends with the biggest breasts.

Fast-forward eight years, and the big ones these days are Twitter and Instagram. Actually—these are probably considered old platforms now; I'm sure there is something newer, hipper, more confusing out there, maybe SnapChat? For the sake of the story, let's just say Twitter is still the hot new thing.

As the seatbelt lights turned off and the flight attendant announced we could turn our phones back on, I took my phone out and purchased the on-air wifi, which was something I usually didn't do out of principle. I hated the thought of not being able to disconnect for a few hours here and there. If anything, I preferred to use the time as an exercise in restraint, which was something I could always use. Once I was online, I opened Twitter and continued to look through Keith's profile. With the same intensity Bill used to look through the latest issue of *SkyMall*, I looked for any signs pointing to what kind of wheelchair guy he was.

I found it.

He had posted a link to an interview, in which he revealed that a skydiving accident had left him a quadriplegic twelve years ago, when he was just twenty-one years old.

Quadriplegic? I couldn't believe it. He had looked so...*normal* when I passed him walking to my seat. I had to google "quadriplegic" to make sure it was the one that affected all four limbs (I'm not in porn because of my smarts). I had never fucked a man in a wheelchair before, much less one who didn't have the use of any of his limbs. How had he tweeted me? Was it possible to lose control of your limbs while retaining control of your hands? It was a universe completely new to me, and it would be a lie to say that I didn't immediately fantasize about him being my first wheelchair guy.

I've always been a fan of first times. When I look back, all of my favorite porn scenes are the ones where I did something for the first time—my first anal scene, for instance. Or my first double penetration scene. My first gangbang. My first gangbang with double anal. My first French kiss in the fourth grade will forever be one of the sexiest moments of all time, even though it was with a nerdy Irish kid with braces who was shorter than me even on his toes. I love firsts so much that there are currently three men out in the world who all believe they were the first to penetrate me. There's a certain rush that comes only with the first time, and then it's lost forever once it's over.

I often wonder how many more of these first encounters I have left. As someone who had already done a good amount sexually, who was now *married*, how much was there really left for me? It's something that doesn't keep me up at night, but once in a while when I'm feeling particularly moody, it makes me kind of sad. Most of the time, I make myself feel better by ordering a pizza and turning on a crime show, thinking how lucky I am to have such mundane problems. I could be a serial murderer, my latest victim on the verge of being discovered by the police. On top of that I could be a parent, and it would be revealed to my children that I'm a demon. What if my fetish was not only to kill, but to kill small children? After raping them. It would make me a number-one target for anal rape in prison. (In this anti-fantasy, I am also...shudder...a man.) Sometimes when I thought of how much worse my life could be, it put things into perspective.

Closing my eyes and leaning my head against the window, I thought about how hot it would be to fuck Keith. There probably wouldn't be that many different options, position-wise, but that was okay. I usually didn't like to be on top, but this would be different. Did his dick work? Maybe he used Caverject, which was a solution that was injected into the base of an impotent penis—I only knew about this because some of the guys in porn used it. Or maybe his dick worked just fine, and I was being ignorant? Who knew? And what would I tell Toni? Outside of porn, we were monogamous—fucking Keith would definitely constitute cheating, which I had never even considered doing in the two years we had been married.

As usual, my mind was escaping logic. The man had merely asked me to sit next to him—not to actually fuck him. Maybe he was married. Maybe he was gay, just a fan of the wit I displayed on my Twitter feed (keep dreaming!). Maybe his dick didn't even work, after all. I let out a sigh and went to sleep.

When I awoke, we were already landing. I grabbed my mirror out of my purse, and made sure I looked presentable. I explained to Bill the situation as best I could.

"What? He's in a wheelchair? On a plane?"

I punched Bill in his arm. "Don't be weird about it." I stood up as the seatbelt light went off, leaving Bill still seated with a confused look on his face. Looking over the seats in front of me, I spotted Keith. He was definitely as cute as I remembered.

When it was my turn to exit, I walked up to his seat. He was in the front row of the plane. I squeezed myself into the space between his legs and the wall.

"Hi, I'm Asa," I introduced myself.

"I'm Keith. I'm a big fan," he smiled and shook my hand. He didn't seem to have any trouble lifting his arm, but when I took his hand, it definitely felt unlike a normal hand...it felt stiff.

"This is my friend Bill," I introduced. Bill shook his hand and looked at me as they touched. I pretended not to notice.

"This is my assistant Roberto," Keith nodded to the man sitting next to him. Roberto nodded back, without saying a word. "Get up, let her sit down," he said in what I took as a rude tone. Roberto did as he said, and I sat down apologizing, embarrassed.

"Can I meet you at baggage claim?" I asked Bill. He looked relieved that I gave him an out. Taking our bags, he left as Roberto took a seat on the other side of the aisle.

"So where are you coming from?"

"A dance gig in Seattle, you?"

"I was at a charity event. Have you ever fucked a guy in a wheelchair?"

I was taken aback by his bluntness; I didn't think the conversation would go there quite so soon. But I stayed seated. "No," I answered. I tried not to smile, but my face failed me.

7

"It works, you know. I'm trying to get sponsored by Viagra. I take one of those things, and it's a party." He was dead serious. He wasn't even smiling.

"Yeah?" I couldn't think of anything else to say. The whole thing was moving too fast—yes, I had already decided this man was fuck-worthy, and yes, he answered the very question I had been pondering, but I thought maybe we would exchange numbers and pretend to be friends first. Besides, I needed time to think of what I would tell Toni. Or would I even tell him at all?

"You know Roxanne?" He suddenly asked. "She's in your line of work."

"Roxanne Summers?"

"Yeah her. I used to mess around with her. You can ask her, she'll give me a good review." Everything he was saying was wrong. He was coming on way too strong, and already name-dropping other porn girls he had slept with? It was so not my style, but somehow it really worked for him. Or maybe I was blinded by the prospect of having another "first." Or maybe it was the grey hoodie. All I could think about was what it would be like to fuck him, and would it be totally wrong of me? How mad would Toni be? Maybe I could convince him somehow that it was something I just needed to get out of my system, which was pretty much how I got anything I ever wanted. Or maybe...maybe I could keep this a secret. Would my conscience allow that?

As if he were reading my mind, he asked, "Is that something you'd wanna try?"

I paused. "Well, the thing is, I'm married." I already felt better about myself.

"That's okay," he smiled. "I have a fiancée."

I couldn't hide the shock on my face, my jaw dropped. What? This man was engaged to be married, and he was hitting on a porn star on a plane?

"So," he continued, "I'll have to keep it a secret too."

"I don't know," I thought out loud. "It's something I'm definitely intrigued by. But I've never cheated on my husband." As the words came out of my mouth, I couldn't help but notice it sounded like a lie. Probably because usually when I started a sentence with the words *I've never*, it usually was a lie.

A flight attendant came up to us. I looked around and noticed the plane was empty.

"We're ready for you, sir," she smiled.

Keith looked annoyed. "Alright," he answered. Without thanking her, he turned to Roberto. "Pay attention," he snapped at him, and turned back to me. "Well it's something to think about. So do you live in LA?"

"I do," I answered. "I grew up in New York, but I live here now. What about you?"

As Keith told me about growing up in California, Roberto came over and in one swoop, picked Keith up like a baby. Keith continued talking to me over Roberto's shoulders, but I couldn't focus—I was too concerned with acting natural.

Just keep looking at his face, keep looking at his face, I chanted to myself as we walked off the plane, Keith in Roberto's arms.

Once he was settled in his wheelchair, we made the long walk through the airport together. Keith used his arms to wheel himself, and again I wondered exactly which parts of his body he had control over. We made the small talk I hated so much, and I was happy to reunite with Bill when we arrived at baggage claim.

"Can I get a picture?" Keith asked once my luggage had come out.

"Of course," I smiled.

"Here dude, make sure it's not blurry," he said, giving his phone to Roberto. "He sucks at taking photos," Keith informed me.

We took the photo, and Keith asked me for my number. Still unsure of where I would take this, I gave him my email address—

the one I used for work. Both of my email accounts forwarded straight to my phone, but I felt less guilty giving him the business one, the one I was looser with.

"What the hell was that?" Bill asked as soon as we got into his car.

"I don't know," I laughed. "I kind of want to fuck him."

"You know you're married, right?" Bill exclaimed. "And *that's* the guy you'd wanna cheat with?"

"You're such an asshole!" I gave Bill a punch in the arm. "Just 'cause he's in a wheelchair?"

"No," Bill said with a bewildered look. "That guy was a total dick."

Bill was right. In the short time I had spent with Keith, I had noticed more than a few red flags—but I was consciously ignoring them.

"Oh, and he's engaged," I remembered aloud. "Isn't that crazy? There's no hope. He's proof that all men cheat. That dude is a quadriplegic, and he *still* cheats."

"So he is a quad?" Bill asked. "When I shook his hand, it was like a dead fish."

"Don't be a dick," I told Bill, but secretly agreed with the comparison.

"And where does this guy even live? Where would you fuck him?"

"He lives in Santa Monica. And I'd probably have to go to him. I mean...he's not coming to my house. I'm married!"

"So basically you mean *I'd* drive you to Santa Monica, wait in the car while you fuck this wheelchair dude, and drive you back?"

"I guess. I wonder if the sex would be good."

"Probably not as good as you're fantasizing."

I looked down at my phone. I had a new email. It was from Keith.

"Oh my god, he just emailed me!" I jumped in my seat.

"How does he even type?" Bill asked as I shushed him, reading the email.

"It was nice meeting you, I'd love to see you soon," I read out loud.

We rode in silence for a bit, and I thought about his fiancée. Had he ever been caught cheating? How long had they been together? My grandfather was paralyzed by a stroke shortly after I was born, and my grandmother had taken care of him for over twenty years before he died.

"Do you think she wipes his ass?" I asked Bill.

As if he had been thinking the same thing, he answered right away with another question. "Can you imagine how she must feel, getting cheated on by a man whose ass she has to wipe?"

"I can't even," I replied in horror.

When we arrived at my house, I got out of the car, still unresolved on whether I would reply to Keith's email or not. Driving away, Bill yelled, "Don't be stupid!"

I walked into the house to find Toni playing a video game on the sofa.

"Hi Ashka," he paused his game to give me a kiss. Hearing the nickname exclusive to my husband made me feel immediately guilty. "How was your flight?"

"There was a fan in a wheelchair," I blurted out. I hadn't planned on saying anything about Keith, but it came out of my mouth before I could do anything about it.

"Ah," Toni grinned. "Let me guess, you wanted to fuck him."

I started to laugh uncontrollably. I wanted to deny it, but I couldn't—I felt I was caught red-handed, even though I hadn't even really done anything. Toni knew me too well—to think I could get away with cheating was a joke. To think I'd even *want* to cheat on a man who knew me so well, and still loved me, was all of a sudden completely absurd. Everything I had been turning over and over in my mind for the past few hours melted away.

"I swear, he was so hot!" I screamed, as I gave Toni a big hug. "But he was SUCH an asshole!"

Toni sighed, smiling. "Ahh, my wife is such a slut."

Here was a man, who knew me more than anybody—more than I gave him credit for. He knew my thought process, he knew how much I thought about fucking everybody that came into my path—and yet, he trusted me enough to know that I wouldn't.

Snuggling into his chest, I felt like the luckiest girl in the world.

I never wrote Keith back (again, sounds like a lie but it isn't) and he still emails me now and again. Although I never reply, I always open it and think about what it would be like to fuck him. And then I get on with my day.

Haiku

Zero cavities
Two abortions, One divorce
Thirty years on earth

Death by H

"Heroin is the most key ingredient to the plan."

"True. And industrialized food. Like Ben and Jerry's."

"I also want to spend all my money. Every last cent."

"Asa. I do not want to die with one penny."

"Maybe even go into debt. So where are we gonna do it again? Or are we gonna travel?"

"The city!"

"But it's so cold..."

"Yeah but it's *our* spot. Plus we don't have to go outside."

"Right, right, we can just get everything delivered. Like a hundred percent of the time."

"It's lazy-friendly. And if Earl is still alive, he can sell us the H."

"Yeah, it's perfect. I'm gonna try to get as rich as possible. So we can get more drugs and food."

"I don't think I'm gonna be rich. I mean I'm still trying to be independent."

"Don't worry, I'm sure we'll have enough."

"I'll never stop trying though. But I won't marry for money. Actually, I won't marry at all."

"Marrying for money is overrated."

"I would marry a doctor for prescriptions."

"Hmm, not a bad idea. Cause marrying a dealer would be too much drama."

"Actually, I would totally marry a doctor. It would be a Jay-Z/Beyoncé type of marriage."

"How long should we go for?"

"Maybe a five-year-plan. I don't know. Are five amazing years better than twenty mediocre ones? Maybe not. But getting old must suck so badly. There's definitely an appeal to dying young. Though, I think I'd make an amazing old person."

"A twenty-year plan is too long."

"No, twenty years is not a plan—it's just life. Five years would be the plan."

"Ha, right. Well I think five great years is better than twenty mediocre for sure."

"I think this may be a way to maximize life. Just be very rational. Look at life like an Excel sheet."

"Do you think five years is even too long?"

"Maybe. Maybe one year is better. A one-year suicide plan could be great."

Some years ago, my best friend Dee and I made a decision. When the time was right, we would take a to-be-determined amount of time to kill ourselves slowly via heroin. Every few months or so, we revisited the idea, adding things and tweaking it to make it the best plan possible. With every celebrity death, we learned something new: Anna Nicole Smith taught us not to mix benzos with our opiates until we were absolutely ready to die; Michael Jackson taught us that even pedophilia could be over-shadowed by untimely death; David Carradine taught us never to masturbate with belts around our necks, because whether people perceived it as a suicide or an accident, it would be equally humiliating. Our plan wasn't something created out of depression, or even a desire for death—it was likely more something born of two control freaks so afraid of painful death and illness, we never even dared *speak* the C-word aloud. And if that did happen—terminal illness, I mean—the plan would obviously be expedited.

Growing up, the first person we ever knew to die in real life, aside from the likes of grandparents and other old relatives, was Chris. Coincidentally, it was due to a heroin overdose. Chris went to school with Dee, and while he wasn't necessarily a part of our group, he came around once every couple of weeks. He was a pothead during the week and did harder drugs on the weekends—just like the rest of us—until one day, when we were seniors in high school, he decided to become a junkie. At that age, none of us had every even considered doing anything harder than cocaine—we did ecstasy, acid, mushrooms, special K, salvia, even the occasional angel dust—but never, ever crack or heroin. In our minds, those drugs were for the homeless. So when one day, Kevin (my ex-boyfriend, who happened to be living with Chris at the time) told us Chris had told him he was going to become a heroin addict, we didn't believe him.

"I swear, he fucking told me he's gonna become a junkie!" Kevin had claimed, but we were sure he was mistaken. Who consciously became addicted to heroin? The very idea was ridiculous.

The next week, Chris came over to Jules's house, where Dee and I had practically lived during our high school years. "Watch," Kevin had told us before he came over—and watch we did. After an hour or so of smoking weed and sitting around Jules's Tribeca triplex, Chris went to the bathroom—for an incredibly long time, probably almost an hour (although, it's hard to tell because I've never been great with the concept of time when I'm high). We sat around and lazily told the others to go check on him, until eventually Jules slowly walked toward the bathroom, sighing with each step. When he came back out a few minutes later, he had a look of disgust on his face.

"Yo, he's just nodding out up there," he explained. "There's literally a needle on the floor."

Chris eventually came back to the living room to join us, and we spent the rest of the evening observing him, judging him, and giving each other wide-eyed looks. We couldn't believe this was someone we knew, our *friend* even. His head nodded up and down as he fell in and out of sleep; when he spoke to us, he would turn his head in our direction, but his eyes would always remain closed. When we went to the stairwell to smoke, his cigarette just hung between his fingers, burning down without him ever taking a puff. I felt sad for him, but at the same time, I couldn't deny he looked like he was having the time of his life, on the inside.

Less than a year later, Chris overdosed. His brother found him on the floor of his apartment. Kevin had already moved out by then, and Chris was living alone. It rocked our worlds. We felt we were too young to know a dead person our age. "There's nothing like being young and seeing death," Jules's father had told us. We nodded in silence, unable to express our feelings—instead, we smoked more weed and wrote our own names over and over on pieces of paper for over an hour. At his funeral, I couldn't even look his parents in the eyes. I silently vowed to never do heroin.

Years later, after I had already started porn, after everyone else had graduated college, after Dee had dated him for two years, Kevin died. It was the morning of my first shoot with Mandingo; I had just prepped my asshole and taken a shower when I got the call—Kevin had overdosed. By then, we all had seen more people in our lives pass, some of us had even lost parents—but Kevin was, and to this day still is, the only one of our group to die. We all handled it in different ways—it's hard to say who took it the hardest. Dee and Kevin had only broken up a few months before, and had he stayed alive, they probably would have been on-again-off-again for at least a few more years. She hasn't seriously dated anyone since, and I don't blame her. Jules knew Kevin the longest, since they were in kindergarten—they even lived under the same roof a few times, and it was possible Kevin was closer to Jules than his own brother. Kevin's death was the only time I'd ever seen Jules cry. As for me, Kevin was my first love. We dated for four years in high school, and when I found out about his death, I went the classic Asian route of denial, moving on to shoot a killer anal scene with Mandingo that day. Then again, maybe it wasn't so classically Asian.

After Kevin's death, I renewed my vow of staying away from heroin. My 2006 and 2007 were years spent high on prescription opiates, but that's the closest I've ever been to the real thing. I can only imagine it's like the best high I've ever felt, times ten. Over the last few years, I've had chances to try it—and although I've been sober since 2008 (please go ahead and roll your eyes at how pretentious that sounds—I know I am), it would be a lie to say I haven't felt tempted. But in the end, I always come back to my promise—heroin is the one drug I'll save for old age. I think of it as my reward for living life. I have no doubt about this plan—if I die in a freak accident before I'm old and wrinkly, you can be sure my last thought will be "...but I haven't even tried heroin." Unless I have yet to fuck a transsexual, in which case, it'll be my second-to-last thought.

The key to this plan, aside from the heroin itself, is the absolute seriousness of it. I've told a few others about it, including my husband, and most everyone seems to see it as a joke. If not that, they think it's something I *think* I'm serious about now, but will eventually change my mind about once I actually reach old age.

A few people have agreed to join in on the pact—Dave, Critter, and David, to be exact—but I can tell they aren't fully committed. First of all, none of us aside from Dee and I seem to agree on what exactly is "old age." Dave thinks sixty is a good age to start, whereas I'm not so sure that's quite old enough. And even if we did agree, Dee and I are a good decade younger than the others. Even if they all are serious, the cards may not line up. And then there's the looming possibility—no, certainty—of terminal illness. To add three more to the pact, statistically, guarantees that at least one of us will need to start the plan early.

The last time we spoke about it, Dee and I agreed the perfect age to start was somewhere around seventy-five. I'm thirty now. If I have kids at say, thirty-five (and that's still a big if), then they in turn will probably have children when I'm sixty, at the earliest. Meaning my heroin journey will start when the grand-children are around fifteen years old, which is a good age as any for a grandparent to die. By then, Toni will probably either have passed (he's ten years older than me) or be old enough that he won't care that his wife is a junkie. He's jokingly entertained the idea of joining in, but if we have kids, I know him well enough to know he won't. Plus, he's always been more of an "upper" kind of guy, which for me, as a pure downer advocate, is a sure sign that I must really, really love him.

Another reason I know that this is the perfect plan is that when I think of my parents taking this route, I feel nothing but relief. After watching all four of my grandparents die, three of them after years of suffering, I'm absolutely certain it is the best way to go, rivaled only by going to sleep one night and never waking up. My grandmother on my mom's side died this way, and even then, she had years of sadness following her husband's death. Had she been getting high all those years, and *then* gone to sleep and never woken up, how much better would the end of her life have been?

I casually mentioned this plan to my mother one day, and surprisingly, she was fully supportive of it—even considered it for herself for a moment, before ultimately deciding it wouldn't be her cup of tea. It was a nice little shock, because my mother has always been highly *un*supportive of my drug use. To this day, if I'm a little tired, or low energy, she will look me in my eyes for some seconds before asking the question: "Are you high?" It annoys me to no end, when she does this—probably because it reminds me of all the times the answer was secretly "Yes," and I had to deal with the guilt and shame that came with it.

The only thing that scares me about this plan is a strong memory I have of when I used to do a lot of Oxycontin. Sometimes, I would be drifting in and out of reality on the Tempur-Pedic mattress my ex and I shared—blackout curtains drawn to block out the daylight, TV blasting *Pardon the Interruption*. My ex Eddie would be awake watching the show as I nodded off— and every so often, I would feel a moment of panic—where I felt I couldn't catch a breath, and I was unable to inhale. It felt something like sleep paralysis, which is about as fearful as a feeling could be. I'd be so high, it would take me a second to lift my arm up and reach out to Eddie—and when I finally did, I'd say with as much urgency as I could, "Put your finger under my nose. Make sure I'm still breathing." Eddie, being used to this, would place his hand by my face and halfheartedly assure me I was still breathing. "If I fall asleep, make sure I don't die," I would tell him just in case, as I drifted off back to being high. Looking back, I wonder if the only reason I felt scared was because I wasn't ready to end my life—there was still so much I wanted to do. To die at twenty-one, with zero accomplishments, high out of my mind next to a man I hated, against a background provided by ESPN, would have been too sad. I wonder if I will feel that kind of panic when I'm high on heroin as an old lady? Did I really feel that anxiety only because I wasn't ready to die? Will I ever *truly* feel ready to die? I've never believed in life after death, so a hell-like post-earth eternity is not something I'm afraid of. Although I'm open to possibilities, I'm pretty sure we just die and that's it—the next batch of babies is born, the human race continues, until one day the sun explodes, or some other natural disaster happens, and it's either back to square one for evolution, or that's it, it's "once upon a time there used to be a planet called earth." Either way, to be honest, I don't really care—I won't be around. For me, this existentialist way of thinking is comforting—it takes the pressure off of being perfect in this life. It makes living not so scary.

In order to avoid the panic I felt back when I was twenty-one, I must do every single thing I want to, before operation heroin. I've done porn, which is probably the biggest regret I would've had, had I not done it. I'd still like to travel more. I'd like to reconcile and develop a closer relationship with my family in Japan. Fucking a chick with a dick is still a must. I need to make Toni happy every day, so that when he looks back in *his* old age, he is happy he spent his life with me. I want to write more books. I want to write short stories. I just want to write—I want to be known as a writer just as much as I'm known for fucking. I want to get fat once. I want to get scarily skinny once too. I want to buy my parents a house. I want to get DP'd by twins. In fact, I need to fuck at least a hundred more people. I want to see a man slip on a banana peel in real life. I want to laugh as much as possible. This plan makes me realize that I do want children after all.

In some ways, I think the only way I'll be able to live a full life is to plan my death fully.

Haiku

Home at six a.m.
Is it still a walk of shame?
I was shooting porn

Ephebophilia

"Okay here's a good one I heard. Would you rather eat a piece of chocolate that tastes like shit, or a piece of shit that tastes like chocolate?"

It was January, and my best friend/porn agent Spiegler and I were driving to Vegas for the most important week in our industry: the annual AVN convention and awards show. Toni had already been there for a week shooting, which worked out, because the four-hour ride was something I looked forward to doing with Spiegler every year.

"Will eating the shit mess up my stomach?"

It was a valid question. I thought about it. "No. In this scenario, eating the shit comes with no medical consequences."

"That's easy, I'd eat the shit."

"Euw!" I excitedly screamed. It was the answer I had been hoping for. I loved debating with Spiegler—his opinion was one I respected above almost anyone's, and it was thrilling when it opposed my own. "But you would *know* it's shit!"

As we went back and forth on whose choice was more valid, my phone started to ring.

Incoming Call from Steve Orenstein

"Hang on, let me get this," I said as Spiegler turned the music down. I had been ignoring most calls for the day, but this was the owner of Wicked Pictures, my boss. "Hey! We're still a couple of hours away."

"Do you know the drama surrounding you right now?"

I quickly tried to think of anything I had done wrong recently. Was I rude to anyone on the set? No. Had I tweeted any rape jokes? No. Did I gossip about the wrong people, *with* the wrong people? Possibly. "No I don't think so... Is everything okay?"

Steve sighed. "I've been with AVN's lawyers all day. Apparently you said something on your podcast that they're not happy with. They're talking about not only canceling your keynote speech, but not having you in the show this year altogether."

I had been chosen as the keynote speaker for this year's show, and it was something I had spent months preparing. It was an honor rarely given to a performer, and I had been (not so) humbly bragging about it to anyone who would listen.

"Was it a rape joke...?" I asked into the phone, looking at Spiegler. He was rolling his eyes. Something I said on the podcast? It could have been anything. "I mean, I say a lot of things on there but it's all meant to be taken..."

"Do you know who Sarah Locks is?"

"Sarah Locks?" At the sound of her name, Spiegler's eyebrows raised. "I know *of* her. She's an insane person, she's always accusing me of being a pedo..." Shit. I knew where this was going. Sarah Locks was a bitter retiree of the industry, who now had a blog and harassed porn stars on social media. She was a known psycho, and no one took her seriously. I had her blocked on all of my accounts. "Fuck. Did she call me a pedophile?"

"Not exactly. She put together a six-minute clip of you saying it's okay for a grown woman to have sex with a fifteen-year-old boy. I just watched the video. Now, I don't know if it's taken out of context, but..."

"That's ridiculous! I mean, come on, isn't that every boy's fanta..."

"I'm gonna stop you right there. Don't say it. I don't wanna hear it. The reason this is such a big deal is that Sarah Locks is now accusing AVN of supporting child pornography."

"What? How did it even go there?"

"All I know is, this Sarah person sounds unstable, but AVN is not pleased."

"Well whatever I said, it was probably taken out of context. I don't know what episode that is, but I've talked about that a few times. I mean...I don't want to say go back to listen to the entire episode in its full context, because I probably said some other horrible shit that they'll like even less." I closed my eyes. I knew the podcast would bring me trouble one of these days.

"So what should I do?" I asked Steve. "We're about two hours away still."

"I'm gonna send you the video now. Call me when you're checked in, and you can come up to the Wicked suite to talk. AVN is probably gonna wanna meet with you."

I hung up and told Spiegler the story. "Sarah Locks? Do they know that bitch is crazy?"

"I don't know if they know. But the damage has been done." I looked out the window and saw that in the midst of this nonsense, we had missed our chance to point out the *Zzyx* sign. "I don't even fuck guys under thirty," I pouted.

The rest of the ride was less enthusiastic. I watched the video Steve sent me, and it was exactly what he had said—a clip of me defending grown women who slept with teenaged boys. I wanted to message Steve to let him know what I was talking about wasn't even pedophilia, it was *ephebophilia*! There was a huge difference, but as Spiegler so kindly reminded me, "This ain't the fuckin' time for that argument."

When we got to the hotel, Toni was already checked into our room. "You're not gonna believe what's fucking going on," I told him.

"What? Already?"

As I told him the situation, I got ready to meet with Steve. "And you know what sucks? This probably means I won't win any awards this year either."

I was always thinking of the important issues.

"Don't worry Ashka, everything will be okay," Toni smiled. "And just so you know, if I were a fifteen-year-old, and a thirty-year-old woman seduced me, it would have been the best thing ever." He paused for a moment before coming to hug me. "Plus, you already have the best award: me."

I could always count on Toni to be on my side.

The (very subjective) truth was, what teenaged boy *wouldn't* think it was the best thing ever? Not that I'd personally be interested in fucking one, nor did I know any women who would, but would being seduced by an older woman *really* be damaging to a fifteen-year-old kid's psyche? I couldn't honestly say I think it would. I did know where AVN was coming from. I knew that, as the industry's possibly most well-known company, they could not support my viewpoint.

I walked across the casino from my room to the penthouse suite Wicked used every year and remembered how much I hated Vegas casinos. Everything was so far apart, and it was guaranteed wherever I was going would be in the farthest tower from the one I was in. Add to this that, starting tomorrow, I'd be in heels.

"Stop," I told myself. "One problem at a time."

Truthfully, it seemed that something crazy happened at every AVN. There was the year I hosted the awards show, and Toni and I got into a huge fight that ended with my face on the ground. My second AVN ever, I almost didn't make the awards show because I had accidentally kissed a guy in front of my then-boyfriend. There was last year, when every girl at the Wicked table was crying for different reasons before the show even started. Then there was that year I got into a fight with Keiran, Brazzers' main contract guy, and they banned me from shooting for them for an entire year. It was the first and only time I had ever fought with someone in the business; it was ironic that it was with Keiran, because he's one of the people I get along with the *most* in porn. Whenever I had gossip, he was the first one I called after Spiegler.

We were hosting a party together for Brazzers, and unaware I had signed a contract stating that was to be the *only* party I hosted that weekend (because really, who reads all that fine print?), I booked two other hosting gigs at two other clubs. Ultimately, I was able to keep all three jobs, but Keiran wasn't happy about it. He kept threatening me that if I didn't drop the other two clubs, I'd never shoot for Brazzers again, which enraged me, because who the fuck was he to tell me that? (It ended up that he *was* totally someone who could tell me that.) It was my fault completely, and I can say that now that it's been four years. At the time, though, I didn't feel that way, and we fought the entire time leading up to the party, on the phone before we got to Vegas, at the convention while we were signing, in the limo ride over to the club, and even on the red carpet taking photos. I look at those photos now and laugh—I went in denim shorts and flat boots, as if I were retaliating against Keiran, when in reality, I just made myself look like an idiot, going to a club dressed like I was heading to a day at Six Flags.

Spiegler had his own share of AVN stories, maybe more than anyone in the business. First of all, a good twenty percent of the girls are under twenty-one—which is the minimum age to do basically anything fun in Vegas. Keeping these girls from getting kicked out of the casino was a task on its own. A few years ago, he bailed two of our girls out of jail for two unrelated events; one girl beat her boyfriend up, another had somehow, in a fit of rage, attacked and destroyed a slot machine. At every AVN, at least one girl got dropped from the Spiegler Agency. A fun game was always predicting who it would be, unless, of course, you ended up as the one getting dropped.

It took me a while to figure it out, but I now know why otherwise-lovely girls turn into raging cunts at AVN. It's no phenomenon; there is a perfectly reasonable combination of explanations:

1) We are fucking starving. The convention starts on a Wednesday and goes through Saturday. Saturday night is the awards show, so all week while we are signing and meeting fans, we are starving so that we can fit into our skintight dresses for the awards.

2) We are fucking exhausted. Typically, a girl's AVN schedule consists of getting into makeup at 7:00 a.m., signing for eight hours straight, rushing back to the room to get touched up, and then going to host a party until 4:00 a.m. Repeat for four days.

3) We are bombarded every time we leave our hotel rooms. I love attention probably more than anyone I know, but AVN is overwhelming even for me. Because the convention and awards show are all at the same casino, everyone—performers, producers, and fans alike—stay in the same building. This is both convenient and irritating; unless you stay in your tiny room, there is zero privacy.

4) Our feet hurt and no one cares. Standing in heels for

twenty hours a day is painful, and it's in these uncomfortable moments that I remember how sexist the world is.

5) We are fucking nervous as fuck. As much as we like to pretend the awards show doesn't matter to us, it does. It fucking does.

Truly a recipe for disaster.

The convention would not start until tomorrow, but already people I recognized as porn fans were wandering around the casino floor. I put the hood of my sweatshirt over my head and walked quickly, looking down at the floor, appropriately playing the role of woman-accused-of-pedophilia-advocacy. I wondered how I would feel if the genders were reversed. Thinking of a grown man sleeping with a fifteen-year-old girl felt, immediately, different and gross. Yet, I had been that girl. Did it damage me? I honestly didn't think so—it was well after I had been fucking boys my own age, and I was emotionally ready. In fact, I'd always felt that there were two kinds of fifteen-year-old girls: ones mature enough to be fucking, and ones who weren't. It would make sense to have some kind of EQ test to be passed along with the drivers permit exam, but I wouldn't be the one suggesting it. Who would I even take such an issue to? Was there some kind of international council of sex? Or would this be a DMV thing?

These were the kind of thoughts I kept in once I was in the Wicked suite. I apologized to Steve for once again being a problem, and we met with AVN, and their lawyers, and their PR team.

Out of respect for AVN, out of appreciation for them allowing me to remain the keynote speaker, out of fear of never winning an award from them again, I won't repeat the dialogue that went on in that suite.

I will say that I repeated the line "I am not a pedophile" at least four times, and that in the end, we came to the agreement that I in fact, was not, and that in the future, I would consider that my words had more weight than I knew.

And I didn't win any awards that year.

HAIKU

GOING COMMANDO
SHAVED MY PUSSY JUST IN CASE
I SHOULD TRIP AND FALL

A Permanent Reminder of a Temporary Situation

I was barely fourteen, and my fake ID wouldn't work there—that very street, St. Marks Place, was where I had gotten it. It was after school, and Dee and I had gone from shop to shop, remaining optimistic while receiving one rejection after another, until finally one Puerto Rican guy didn't care to check how old I was.

"I only take cash," were the first words he spoke to us. He was bald, short, covered in tattoos, but not threatening. If anything, he was the opposite; his failure to ask for my ID seemed a lazy move, rather than an advantageous one.

As if paying with credit card were a choice, I agreed to pay in cash.

"Well what do you want?"

I looked around the walls...not technically walls, this was not technically a shop. It was more of a booth; the street was lined with a dozen or so of them. They all sold the same things: body jewelry, hair clips, bongs, tattoos.

"I'm not sure," I answered, looking at what were clearly photocopies of photocopies. "I have forty dollars. What can I get for that?"

"That's all you got?" he laughed. "For that, I can give you a heart or a star. Not no big one, neither."

I turned to Dee. "What do you think?"

"Definitely a star," she said. "You're gonna regret a heart when you get old."

"Okay, lemme get a star," I told the guy, and took my forty dollars out of my North Face asspack.

I was seventeen. My boyfriend at the time, Kevin, drove me to New Jersey in his dad's car. His dad didn't allow Kevin to drive, but once a week or so, we slipped the parking attendant twenty dollars, and he would pull the car out for us.

I had searched "permanent makeup nyc" on Craigslist, and while hers was not the first name to come up, she was the closest to the city, and based on my feeling, the least likely to ask about my age. We went into her basement, which makes the situation sound much shadier than it actually was. Or maybe it *was* that shady, and I just wanted my eyeliner tattooed on that badly. Kevin watched *The Simpsons* on the sofa as the lady put numbing cream on my eyelids. I could hear it was the episode where Maggie was going to say "Dada" for the first time.

"Will I be able to wear makeup tomorrow?" I asked.

"No," she replied. "You won't want to wear any kind of eye makeup for at least a week. I'll give you an after-care pamphlet before you leave."

Even with the numbing cream, it was painful, much more painful than the star on my forearm. Tears involuntarily spilled out of my eyes as I apologized, fearing it would make the process harder for her.

"Don't worry," she smiled. "You just stay still."

We drove home in silence as I held a bag of frozen peas on my eyes. Kevin didn't need to say anything; I knew he thought I was ridiculous.

Kevin is dead now, and my tattooed eyeliner is long gone—it faded slowly over the years, and there's no trace of it now. I miss them both, but I can only get one back.

I had just turned nineteen. It was my first time in Las Vegas, my first time taking a prescription opiate, and my first time getting married. High and happy, I signed a waiver promising that I wasn't on any drugs. We were two weeks into our relationship; we were two weeks into knowing each other, and the night before, we had participated in a drive-through wedding in the backseat of Mike's car.

"Wouldn't it be hilarious if we got married today?" he had asked.

And I had agreed.

It was now four hours before our flight back to NYC, and we were walking around a casino, enjoying our new titles as husband and wife. We passed a tattoo shop. "I wanna get a tattoo!" I exclaimed. "I'll get one too," he answered.

He went first. He got my name tattooed on his back. "What if we break up?" I asked. In my opiated logic, I felt the chances for regret were higher for a tattoo than a marriage.

"A tattoo is a permanent reminder of a temporary situation," he smiled.

"That's not an answer..."

When it was my turn to sit in the chair, the artist asked me what I wanted. I pointed to a picture of a naked lady on the wall.

I was still nineteen. I was still high on opiates; I had been every day since the drive-through wedding. Although I had done drugs throughout high school, I had somehow managed to stay away from prescription painkillers, until Eddie. He opened me up to a new world—no longer did I want acid, or ecstasy, or cocaine, or even my favorite ketamine; all I wanted was to feel the warm happiness Oxycontin brought me.

The worst part of an opiate habit is the irritability it brings; because of this, we constantly fought. Every day was another unnecessary fight—he hurt my feelings by making a certain facial expression, or he was mad at me for getting too high and making a mess in his friends' country house. We fought not just at home but everywhere—our friends knew that hanging out with us was a gamble. If we all drove someplace together, there was a good chance we would fight, and getting home would mean finding another means of transportation for half the group.

This time, we had been in the car. He pushed me out of it while it was moving, in broad daylight in the middle of Soho—I don't deny I deserved it; I was punching him while he was driving, causing the car to swerve in and out of our side of the street. I walked home sobbing, running away from pedestrians trying to help.

The best moments of our relationship always followed fights like these, and this time was no different. I took another Oxy, we swore to be together forever, and I left the house telling him I'd have a surprise for him when I got back.

Dee sat with me as the man prepared the needle. "Are you sure?" she asked. "You guys were just breaking up an hour ago…"

"I can always cover it up," I shrugged, as the man tattooed Eddie's name on my ankle.

I was around twenty-one. No, I was twenty, definitely twenty. For certain, I had been high on Oxy every day for over a year. We were at Mike's house, his cousin the tattoo artist was in town from Los Angeles. He was tattooing us all. I had chosen two flowers from a Japanese vase in Mike's house for my shoulders.

"You need to put her in rehab," Mike said right in front of me. I wasn't sure if he knew I heard.

I scratched my face and didn't say anything.

I was twenty-four. In porn for a little over a year, divorced for a little over three. I was sober now, living in Los Angeles, and honestly happy. I went to Mike's cousin's shop, the one who had tattooed me last when I was high.

He laughed when he saw me. "I walked into the kitchen, and you were getting your butthole fingered," he said in a pothead drawl.

"I don't remember that," I replied. It was the truth.

"Do you still talk to him? I heard you guys broke up."

I shook my head. "I think he's in jail. I'm actually here because I want this covered up." I pointed to my ankle.

"That's why I never do names," he sighed.

I was twenty-seven. Sober for over four years, I was at the height of my porn career and in the best shape of my life, both physically and mentally. Toni had kept telling me he had a surprise for me—and I had assumed he was going to propose. It's what I wanted, badly; we had been together almost a year, and I was enamored. But when he showed up in New York City where I was visiting my family, with my name tattooed on his wrist, I realized a proposal was not the surprise I had been hoping for.

But then, a few days later, he got down on his knee at Rock-efeller Center and asked me to marry him. "Your parents already know," he beamed after I said yes. He had asked them for my hand in marriage the night before, which meant even more to me than the tattoo and the proposal combined. Yes, this is how two whores who met in a DP scene got engaged.

We were married a week later. It was my second wedding in Las Vegas. An Elvis led the ceremony.

Some days after that, back in LA, I tattooed Toni's name on my wrist.

This time, Dee didn't ask me if I was sure.

Besides, I could always get it covered up.

I am thirty. Perhaps the most profound tattoo is the figurative one on my forehead. It will not fade over time, I cannot cover it up, it cannot be removed, and it is more hindering than if it were literal. It is the one guaranteed permanent thing in my life: my porn career. When I walk on the street, the strangers I pass have seen my most private moments. When I eat at a restaurant with my parents, fellow diners are shocked that I am somebody's daughter. If I have my own children, their friends' parents will be wary of letting their kids come over for a playdate.

I have been lucky. My porno tattoo has been worth it. I wouldn't trade it for any amount of money in the world, for any other experience, for any kind of love.

But I cannot help but feel saddened for girls with the same scarlet letter who want it to fade over time, want it covered up, want it removed.

Haiku

Bruised knees cramp my style
They scream "cheap whore" when I am
An expensive one

(Probably Bad) Relationship Advice

I'm no relationship expert. First of all, I'm too young; thirty is hardly old enough to be an expert on anything as complicated as love, really. Second, I've been married twice, engaged thrice, and my longest relationship so far is with my dog. My second longest was with my high school boyfriend, who later dated my best friend, and (on an unrelated note) is now dead. Most of my adulthood has been spent in a series of one-year relationships, generally expiring because I got bored, or they left me because I am a terrible person to be with.

Additionally, another reason why I am no expert is that I'm currently in the most successful relationship I've ever had, and it's still only been less than four years. But this is about four-hundred percent the length of my usual relationships, so even if we got divorced tomorrow, I'd still consider it a great victory. Therefore, I'll offer some advice.

1) SEPARATE BEDROOMS
Toni and I don't share a bedroom, or a bathroom, or an office, or

phone chargers, or a pizza. The first one is key, I think. Like many constructive steps in a relationship, this started with me throwing a stone Buddha statue at Toni's head. It was in the first year of our cohabitation, before we had gotten married—and we had gotten into an argument about the dishes. Yes, the dishes. It's important to fight about these little things in the beginning, I believe—to set the rules for the future. (More on this later.)

Growing up in New York City, I never had a dishwasher. While many apartments come with these futuristic machines installed now, when I was a kid living with my parents, they did not. And later, when I became an adult, being able to afford a New York City apartment on my own with one was just laughable. So for these reasons, when I moved to LA and rented an apartment with a dishwasher, I just washed the dishes like I was used to and used the machine as a drying rack. This system worked great, especially for a single woman who ate only salads and lived alone.

Toni moved in, and like a normal human being, was not accustomed to this genius alternative use for the dishwasher. Although I told him at the very early stages of our relationship about my method, he constantly forgot, and placed his dirty dishes in the machine, with my clean dishes. Thinking of the molecules from his dirty dishes migrating over to my clean dishes was not something I could let go of easily. I would remind him, he would feel that I was nagging, and we would fight. He would agree to be more mindful, I would agree to be more understanding, and we would make up.

This one particular time, though, we couldn't seem to make up. Like many fights, it turned into a fight about the fight. I cried to Toni that "forgetting" my method just meant he didn't respect me enough to remember. He in turn suggested I was menstruating (his word, not mine—remember, I am married to a foreigner), which understandably made me morph into a psychotic monster. I jumped on him and started to punch him, he threw me off, and like the gentleman that he is, he stormed into the guest bedroom to avoid hitting me. I banged on the wooden door until it cracked, at which point he called me a crazy bitch, came out of the room, and yelled at me for destroying my own living quarters. If there is one thing that will make me crazy, it's calling me crazy. So I took the stone Buddha statue next to me, which was heavy enough that I had trouble holding it, and threw it at his head. He ducked, pointed his finger at me, and yelled that I was fucking lucky he ducked. (I'll give it to him, he was right. That time.) He grabbed me by my hair, so I tried to get away, and ended up on the floor punching his legs. He dragged me by my hair into our bedroom, picked me up by my neck, and threw me onto the bed. "You fucking stay there you stupid bitch," he pointed at me again, and went to the guest room and locked the door. I was honestly a bit tired from the whole fiasco, so instead of pursuing the matter further, I stayed in bed crying all night and feeling sorry for myself.

The next morning, I awoke with a fresh mind. As much as I hated to admit it, I felt ashamed of my behavior the night before, which was only accentuated when I walked out into the living room and saw the shattered Buddha on the floor. Toni was nowhere to be seen. I cleaned up the mess I had made, and the entire apartment, and was embarrassed to see the dent in the hardwood floor that would now be there forever, a permanent reminder that I had sort of tried to kill my boyfriend.

Toni came home later that day, and I apologized. He apologized too, and after a couple days of being silent toward each other, and a couple nights of sleeping apart, the fight ended the usual way, with him agreeing to be more mindful of my dishwashing method, and me agreeing to be more understanding of his forgetfulness. We had make-up sex, and as with most fights, came out stronger than ever, more in love than ever.

That night though, after we had spent the day being sweeter

to each other than ever, after having sex like nine hundred times, I couldn't help but notice how much nicer it had been to sleep alone. As we lay in bed together, side by side, I noticed that even in our king-sized bed, we kept kicking each other by accident, waking each other with every movement, every groan. I let it go, thinking this was the cost of being in a loving relationship.

The next night, as we each read our own books on opposite sides of the bed, I wondered why couples even had to sleep together. If I were alone right then, I could sprawl out diagonally and not be awakened every time he got up to pee. I turned to Toni. "I feel like it was kind of nice, sleeping in separate rooms."

"Thanks god you said something!" Toni exclaimed. (Again, married to a foreigner.) "I felt so good sleeping alone."

"Should we just...sleep apart? Is that weird?"

And so it was decided, and we never looked back. When we purchased a house two years later, we didn't for one moment consider that we might share a bedroom again. As we looked at open house after open house, we each declared which room would be "my room" and argued who deserved which room more, before ultimately deciding on a four bedroom, three bath, where we could each have not only our own bedrooms and bathrooms, but offices too. When we moved in, we each decorated our rooms very differently, taking pride and challenging guests to say whose room looked better. (Mine, obviously.)

People are confused when we tell them about our sleeping arrangement. "Are you guys in love? Do you still have sex? Is this a green-card marriage?" they'll ask, and I don't blame them. It's unconventional. We are in love, we do have sex, and this isn't a green-card marriage. We spend every evening together like any normal couple, but when it's time to go to sleep, we each get ready for bed in our own bathrooms, and then he comes to my room to tuck me in, we spend about ten minutes winding down, and then he goes to his room, and then we see each other in the morning. I love this. I love that we are okay with this. I love having my own space, that I decorated my room exactly how I wanted, and that if I choose to stay up all night reading or masturbating or writing, I could do so without bothering him. I love that I can sleep in my ideal temperature (hot as balls) and he can sleep in his (cold as fuck.) I love that all of my belongings are in my own area of the house, and I love that I have a place that is only mine. Maybe it's the only child in me. But Toni isn't an only child, and I know he loves it too. When we go on vacation, we sleep together, but we both laugh at how nice it is when we come home to our separate bedrooms. When we awake in the morning, we are excited to see each other, and I give him a big hug, genuinely asking how he slept.

2) FIGHT A LOT IN THE FIRST YEAR

Like what we now refer to as the Buddha incident, try to fight a lot in the first year. Go ahead and be petty—if you're going to spend a significant portion of your life with someone, they may as well know how you like things done. This applies not only to household chores like how to properly use a dishwasher, but sex, pet peeves, the definition of "cheating"...everything, really. In that first year of living together, Toni and I constantly fought about everything, many (if not most) of the fights being repeats. Eventually, we learned to conclude an issue forever by this very simple algorithm: Whoever cares more about the matter gets their way.

One particular issue that came up more than most for us was where the lines were drawn when it came to work. Being that our jobs are to fuck people besides each other, the rules of dating were not as clear-cut as, say, in a traditional monogamous relationship. Can we fuck people outside of porn? Can we fuck someone that we are working with that day when the camera isn't rolling? Can we work with our exes? Can we still perform any sex act we want on camera, or are there certain acts

47

that are now exclusive to home sex?

I've seen it done all different ways, the porno relationship. Some girls don't kiss on the mouth. Some dudes refrain from working with the same girl more than once a week. Some couples only have anal sex with each other. I've learned not to judge any of these decisions—everyone draws the line somewhere different, and however ridiculous it may seem to me personally, I can't knock how someone feels. I can't argue about what's important to somebody.

For me, I don't care what Toni does on the set. I know what kind of male performer he is: He's the guy who tries to fuck the girl while she is still in the makeup chair, before they even start shooting. He's the guy who will keep fucking the girl even when the camera stops rolling. If there is a girl who wants to fuck him on a day when he is just directing, I'd be a fool to think he wouldn't jump at the opportunity. Toni loves his job, and I want him to have a great time when he's at work—I would imagine this is how any woman feels about her husband.

However—anything away from the set kills me. If Toni takes a girl to eat after their scene, I die of jealousy. This is something we fought about constantly in the beginning—and in the end, he realized that going to lunch with a girl meant more to me than it did to him. The level of hurt it caused me outweighed his desire. So on that one, I got my way.

Before you assume I always get my way, let me give an example of a time when Toni got his way.

I love licking men's assholes. It's not the taste, texture, or anything weird or gross like that—I just love watching a man's face when I go there. It always catches him by surprise, and for a millisecond, you see him enter another realm of pleasure. It's not the same with girls, because we are used to having our assholes eaten pretty much every time we have sex—it's much less special.

Toni knew this little tidbit about me, because he'd worked with me before we dated, and he'd watched me work with other guys too. So when we started to get serious, he told me he would rather I abstain from eating men's assholes at work. Women, he said, were fine—his reasoning was that boys had dirty buttholes, while girls had clean ones—while he had no problem kissing me after my tongue had been on a woman's butthole, he did not feel the same if it had been on a man's. Of course, this sounded silly to me. I lightheartedly agreed, with little intention of following through. I figured I'd just do it a little less.

A few months later, I came home from work and was about to get in the shower when Toni angrily brought me his laptop.

"What is this?" he demanded.

I only had to look at the screen for one moment before I knew what he was talking about. In my defense, I was putting a dildo in a guy's ass—I wasn't gonna put it in dry; I wasn't heartless! Of course I was going to lick his butt. I argued this point to Toni, but he wasn't hearing it. We argued for a while before I realized I was arguing for a matter of principle, while he was genuinely upset—the level of his distaste (ha!) for the act trumped my level of desire to perform it. So he won, and I never ate a guy's asshole again.

3) AFTER THAT FIRST YEAR OF FIGHTING A LOT, PICK YOUR BATTLES.

This tip is really just an extension of the last tip. Maybe it shouldn't even be its own thing—but fuck it, I will just make it short.

Once we spent that first year fighting over every petty thing, we learned which issues were truly important and which were not worth fighting over. I no longer use the dishwasher as a drying rack. He no longer goes to lunch with girls. I refrain from licking men's assholes, and he refrains from smoking in the house. We honestly hardly fight anymore, and I really do credit it to the fact that we got all our fighting out of the way in the first year. We know what matters to each other, and we respect it. When something bothers me, I try to think of it like this: Is this worth starting an argument over? In the grand scheme of things, does this really matter? For example, when Toni leaves his socks turned inside out when he throws them in the hamper, it annoys me, because then when they come out of the dryer and I am folding his laundry, it is one extra step to turn them out the right way. But I don't bring this up. This is not worth a fight—it's only one small extra step for me. Him feeling nagged is not worth it. I'd rather save it for an issue that *really* matters to me—one that actually affects my feelings.

4) HAVE YOUR OWN LIFE

Whenever people are like "I married my best friend!" I barf in my mouth a little. Just kidding, because I have no gag reflex. But really, though, I don't think this is a good idea. I've been in relationships before where our social lives were completely intertwined, my friends were his friends, his favorite activities were my favorite activities, and we did everything together. This is all great in the very beginning of the relationship when you just want to spend every second together, but try to avoid it, because once you're past that stage, you're going to want your own social life. Nothing will make you feel more trapped than when you share everything; it's important to have places to go when you don't want to be with that person. Go to separate gyms. Have separate friends. Have hobbies that are your own. Plus, people respect independence; it's important that your partner know that you can live a life without them, that if they treat you like shit, you're able to easily leave and move on with your life. (Unless you have kids, 'cause then you're just fucked.) If your whole life revolves around them, you'd better believe they'll eventually take it for granted.

5) PUT YOUR BEEF WITH OLD-FASHIONED, PRECONCEIVED GENDER ROLES ASIDE ONCE IN A WHILE AND BE A 1950s HOUSEWIFE

Trust me on this one, the benefits outweigh the pain in your soul.

When we first started dating, like any new couple, Toni and I went out to eat most nights. Consequently, I gained eight pounds, he gained twelve, and being in a business where our paychecks depended on our looks, we mutually decided something should probably be done about this. For the most part, a man who watches what he eats is a big turn-off for me, but if his money depends on it, I can live with it. In my mind, we had come to the conclusion that I would go back to eating fruits and salads, and he would go back to his chicken and brown rice, or whatever he made for himself during the five years he was single. This lasted for about a month before he casually mentioned one day, "So, when are you gonna make that dinner for me?"

Naturally, as I always did when asked something I wasn't confident about, I immediately got defensive. "What dinner? What are you talking about?"

"You said you were gonna make me dinner," Toni smiled. "Remember? When we decided to start eating healthy?"

There was no way in hell I had promised him that, because I would never have made such an idiotic promise, since I didn't know how to cook. It was a skill I was confident I could learn if needed, but it was something I had never been interested in. If anything, I was sort of against cooking for a man *in principle*— why should *I* be the one cooking? Why not him? But this was the beginning of the relationship, before I had let my crazy out, when I was still shaving above the knees on a regular basis. I was still trying to sell the idea of the perfect girlfriend.

"Okay, how about tomorrow?" I answered in my best nonchalant voice. And so it was decided.

The next day, I went to the grocery store straight after my shoot. I had shot a gonzo scene, where the plot was basically me and my cocksman of the day sitting in a room naked, the script consisting of one line: "I've been waiting for you." It was a quick day. With cum in my hair and my eyeliner smeared, I looked through recipes on my phone and walked into the store. As people walking by complained I was in their way, I wondered if I should just Mrs. Doubtfire it and order some delivery and serve it as home cooking. I quickly decided this was a bad idea, as my ex-boyfriend Luke had done that very thing to me a few years back—resulting in a huge fight. "Why would you leave the containers in the house?" I had yelled. "If you're gonna do something this stupid, at least make sure I don't find out!" Looking back, the act alone probably didn't deserve such a reaction—but Luke was a pathological liar, and this was just one in a string of many lies I had caught him in.

I decided on making salmon with a side of mashed sweet potatoes, along with a kale salad. I wasn't sure if fish and sweet potatoes went well together, and I was pretty certain Toni had specifically told me once he didn't like salad, but these were the only three items I had ever prepared in my life, so I figured it was the safest bet. Besides, the meal would a good balance of carbs/protein/fat, and maybe that would make him realize that one day, after I was done sucking dicks on camera, I'd make an excellent mother.

When I got home with the ingredients, I got into the shower and repeated the phrase "domestic goddess" over and over in my mind as I washed the dried cum out of my hair. The stove hadn't even been turned on yet, but I felt like the best girlfriend in the world. Work all day, come home, cook a nice meal for my man— was this...was this the new me? I briefly considered going back out to buy a cute apron, but it was getting late and Toni would be coming over soon.

This story would be much funnier if the dinner had been a disaster, but the truth was that it went very smoothly, and Toni even asked for a second serving (which was actually in itself a disaster, because now this was something he might expect). (I had forgotten an important rule I had been applying to life ever since I read it in a cartoon as a child: If you don't want to do something, do it poorly the first time, and no one will ever ask you to do it again.) What followed dinner was the best sex I'd ever had. And for the next week, he showed up with random surprises—he even got me one of those surprise-pearl things I had always wanted (no, not a pearl necklace, although actually, he probably gave me one of those too), where you get to crack open the oyster and see what kind of pearl was inside.

Thinking I had fulfilled my proof-of-cooking-skill duties, I didn't cook again, not a single time, for years to follow. Instead, it became a running gag that in all the time we had been together, I had only cooked for Toni once. And this is where this anecdote takes a turn for the worse. Every time Toni would jokingly tell this story, and end it with the punchline of me never cooking again, the feminist in me would come out and I'd become enraged. "I'll cook for you when you pay all the bills and I can stay home on drugs in my pajamas all day," I'd yell. Of course, this was not what either of us wanted—while I don't judge it, I'd been a stay-at-home wife before, and that life just wasn't for me. "Why don't YOU cook for ME?" I'd scream. "You think my role is to cook for you just because I'm a WOMAN?" Toni would calmly explain over and over, no, that was not the case. He wanted me to cook because it made him feel loved and cared for.

It took years for me to finally hear this.

Nowadays, I cook once a week, and not because I'm the woman. I do it because I want to make him happy. The days I cook are the days that Toni is the sweetest to me. And when he's a dick, I can throw it in his face and say things like "And to think I spent all fucking day COOKING FOR YOU!" It's a win-win.

6) TAKE THAT FIVE-LANGUAGES-OF-LOVE TEST

I only recently found this test. It was brought to my attention by Bill Poon, my friend/driver, and not the other way around. It sounds silly, but I truly believe this test has brought me a greater sense of what Toni needs to be happy, and vice versa.

The premise is that there are five languages or expressions of love, and different ones resonate strongly with each of us. They are: quality time, (tangible) gifts, words of affirmation, acts of service, and physical touch. Toni scored the highest in words of affirmation and quality time. It made me realize how, while we spend lots of quality time together, it was equally important for Toni to hear me say encouraging things, how that is something he equated with being loved—which is something I never would have realized, since I scored extremely low in that category. I am big on giving gifts (it is, shamefully, my highest-scoring language), and I came to realize that instead of focusing so much on giving him lavish gifts (which I do often), it would mean more to him that I tell him verbally how much I appreciate him, how proud I am of him as my husband, how much I love him. Additionally, it made *his* words of affirmation to *me* seem so much more important— because this was his main language of love, I realized how much it meant when he said these things to me.

Ironically, physical touch was the lowest-scoring category for both of us. Which, thinking about it, makes sense—as porn stars, we fuck different people every day. While it's still a highly emotional experience for me, and I do feel a strong sense of lust and love while doing a sex scene, it's not something I hold exclusively for my significant other. It's definitely not the most important thing that defines love for me—I'd much rather give/receive gifts and acts of service. For me, doing a favor for someone is much more intimate than fucking them—and I think realizing this has made Toni appreciate it more when I go out of my way to do something for him. And it's made him more conscious of doing the same for me. Just knowing each other's way of loving has made our relationship stronger.

Haiku

Ancient whore secret:
To give enjoyable head,
Enjoy. Giving. Head.

Black Magic

"She don't want to stick. The girls are very very stubborn, sometimes. Just like human."

I turned my head slowly to Elena, careful not to move the magnets under my neck. "You can tell whether they're boys or girls?"

"Yes. Well actually, they're hermaphrodite. When they first hatch, they are boys. Then, they grow up to be girls," she explained in a Russian accent.

"So when they reproduce, it's like a young boy with a grown woman?"

"Exactly, yes," she laughed. "They cougars."

It was three days before I was to get fucked by eight guys for my next big movie; I was laying on a massage table in a basement in the Pacific Palisades with my arms up over my head, leeches on my skin, sucking my blood. After extensive scientific (aka Internet) research, I had learned this method had been used since ancient times to make bruises disappear faster—up to fifty percent faster. Having spent the last week taking pineapple enzyme supplements, lathered in arnica, and walking around with my arms wrapped in heat compresses, this was the last thing left to try. And with my first gangbang in two years quickly approaching, I was desperate. Elena's website was the first to come up when I searched "leeches" with my zip code.

"Do you think it's gonna work?" I asked as she continued to force the stubborn black worm on my arm. I sounded pathetic even to my own ears; I couldn't believe I was there. But if my bruises didn't fade by Tuesday, the director would be very mad. I only shot one movie a month—it wasn't much to request that I be bruise-free for those few days.

"Ah! There we go!" she exclaimed, just as I felt a pinch on my arm. "I knew she was hungry. Yes honey, it should work. Everybody different—but you should have lot less bruising by Tuesday. This also detoxify your blood. Any other problem you have? Stomach? Heart? Tell me now and maybe we can fix."

I chewed my lip; I did, in fact, have another problem. There was a minor yet stubborn irritation on my nipple that had been coming and going for several months. Four doctors had failed to identify it, much less cure it—I had undergone two rounds of antibiotics before discovering it wasn't an infection, an ultrasound before discovering it wasn't cancer, and even a dairy-free diet before giving up and just living with it. I explained the situation to Elena. "We do muscle testing," she answered matter of factly. "Extra sixty dollars okay?" I figured I was already there, so why not.

What proceeded was something even more ridiculous than putting leeches onto my arms. Elena strapped me into some shoes that looked like they belonged on a horse, shook my legs, and tapped my feet together. "May I have permission to heal your body?"

I looked up to see if she was asking me. Just as I was about to say yes, she held my legs up to show me. "See? Your legs are the same length. This mean yes." I put my head back down and closed my eyes. What the fuck had I gotten myself into?

"Is it a virus?" She asked aloud and shook my legs. This time, I stayed put. "Aha! It isn't. See?" She lifted my legs up, and sure enough, one leg was shorter than the other. "This mean no."

After a round of questioning and shaking my legs, she concluded it was bacteria.

It was quite relaxing really, and I had almost fallen asleep. When I opened my eyes, Elena was standing by my head now with a sheet of paper. "You read these out loud to me. A list of bacterias."

"Me?" I looked at the list. It read like a passage from *Harry Potter*. "I don't think I can pronounce half of these."

"That's okay. You just do your best."

As I went down the list, announcing things like "*Myxococcus xanthus*," "*Bordetella pertussis*," and "*Staphylococcus aureus*," I wondered if I was secretly being tricked into casting a spell on myself. Elena shook my legs after each bacterial name until we came upon one she was satisfied with. Nodding her head, she placed magnets all over my body, clipping them to my clothing.

"Okay sweetie, I leave you here with the magnets and my babies now, I'll be back in twenty minutes. Focus on healing. Getting rid of the bacteria, and letting the babies heal bruises." I promised her I would, and she walked out of the room, presumably upstairs to her husband whom I had passed by on entering the house.

I looked around the room, careful not to move the magnets and leeches strategically placed all over me. There were crystals and plants and drawings of symbols I had never seen. Books with titles like *Quantum Healing* and *Diary of a Yogi*. I couldn't help but keep thinking the words *black magic*.

How did I end up here? Not here, as in the Pacific Palisades, I knew how I had gotten here, by driving for over an hour in traffic. Not here, as in this situation; I knew I was here because I was stupid enough to get a procedure done on my arms a week before a shoot—which I knew would leave marks, because I had gotten the fat-freezing procedure done before. How did I end up here, the proverbial *here*, in this state of constantly trying to change my body? Certainly, being on camera was a big part of it. I was continuously forced to see myself, and critiquing my body was impossible to avoid. Then there was just the fact of being in Los Angeles in general—the superficiality capital of the world. A "10" anywhere else in the country was a Los Angeles "6." And as much as I hated to admit it—the profession I chose, the business I loved so much—was full of young girls, ripe and new, as I only grew older, more washed up, closer to inevitable retirement. Every day, a girl turned eighteen; and every day, I was one day older.

I took a deep breath, closed my eyes, and exhaled as I wondered how much time had passed. Probably less than two minutes. I thought back to a week ago, the day that was the cause of all this mess.

"So that's Juvederm on the bridge of your nose, Botox on your forehead, ultrasound on the jawline, correction of the lips, and cool sculpt on the arms," the doctor had confirmed, the corners of his lips turning up as the rest of his face stayed frozen.

It sounded like a lot more than what I had wanted. "Wait, but is there a way to do all of this without bruising? I don't want my husband to know I'm doing any of it."

The nurse chuckled. The doctor shook his head. "Unfortunately, I can't guarantee you won't have swelling or bruises. If you do, it usually subsides within two weeks."

"Two weeks?" I sat up. "That's crazy." I thought about it. I was shooting in seven days—oh well, I'd just hope for the best that I'd heal in time. As for Toni, he would just have to accept me as I was. Or rather, as I was about to be. "Alright, let's just go ahead and do it."

"Great!" The doctor turned the corners of his lips up again. "I'll have Nancy draw up the paperwork and take your payment. Then we can get started."

If anything, I should have just gotten the nose, the jaw, the forehead, and the lips; I could have saved my arms for *after* the shoot. I'd have an entire month to recover before my next movie. But of course, I was in a rush to lose that fat on my arms. "I bet it'll heal faster than two weeks," I irrationally convinced myself. I was rarely an optimist unless I was doing something bad.

I didn't always care this much about my appearance. Before starting porn, before moving to Los Angeles, I was quite content with the way I looked. There were countless things about myself I was insecure about, but when it came to looks, I was comfortable—or rather, it was something I didn't give much thought to.

Growing up, the women in my family were always on this diet, that diet, participating in different revolutionary workout activities, trying creams and lotions that promised to reverse the signs of aging—had all that subconsciously affected me? In general, my family was overweight. My uncle, in his youth, was a sumo wrestler—which sounds like both a racist joke and a fat joke, but it's just a fact. I was always marveled over as a child; "thin like a swan," my relatives would all say in Japanese.

In school, no one ever commented on my aesthetics—I never felt exceptionally fat, thin, ugly, beautiful, or anything aside from just normal. Dieting was a completely foreign concept to me; I barely worked out, and I never watched what I ate. I wore makeup, but not a lot. I did my hair, but without products. The only cosmetic procedure I had ever done was a boob job for my twenty-first birthday—and really, who didn't want bigger tits—I found people who obsessed over their weight/skin/face a bit trivial. I didn't consider myself anything above average, but I felt hot enough for guys to like me, and that was enough.

When did it change? It's hard to pinpoint when it started, the self-hatred. Was it gradual? It must have been.

Shortly after getting my breast implants, I became a regular on a radio show called "Bubba the Love Sponge." It all came about in a strange way—I was stripping at the Hustler Club in New York City, where I saw a posting in the locker room:

WANTED:
Girls to promote HUSTLER CLUB
NYC on the "Bubba the Love
Sponge" radio show.
Compensation: 3 free house fees

I had never listened to the show, but I knew it aired on Howard Stern's channel on Sirius. As a fan of radio and free house fees (on an average night, it cost five hundred dollars to dance at the club), I volunteered right away. I did a live interview on the show, they loved me, and within a few months, I moved down to Florida where they were based to be a regular on the show. In addition, they sponsored my first baby step into porn: a solo-masturbation pay site (i.e., I was naked and masturbating on camera, but not fucking other people).

In the year I was on the show, I gained thirty pounds. "We met you as a hot Asian, but now you're a Samoan giant," they joked on air. Off air, they suggested I sign up for a gym, which at the time also sounded like a joke. I laughed along, agreeing that I had gained weight—but it truly, honestly didn't bother me. As a full-on sufferer of body dysmorphia now, it's hard for me to believe that last sentence; if someone said that to me today, I would stop eating for days. But back then, the comments on my weight were mere observations; if anything, I felt the extra thickness made me sexier. My ass was full, my tits were bigger, and I felt I exuded more *woman*.

I entered the porn industry at 130 pounds, which for my height of five-foot-two is nine pounds over the healthy weight range. No one—not producers, fans, or colleagues—commented on my weight. No one suggested I shed any pounds, and I continuously got compliments on my butt, which was ample for someone of Asian descent. Proud of this asset and happy to be called *thick*, I didn't think twice about losing any weight. In fact, it was the most proud I had ever felt about my looks.

This confidence was short-lived. Like I said, I can't pinpoint exactly when I lost it. But I did. Watching myself on the screen, I noticed things about my body I never had before: a fold in my waist, dimples in my thighs, and was that—no, it couldn't be—a double chin? Where there had never been problems before, I suddenly saw nothing but flaws.

It started with just five units of Botox. Watching myself give an upside-down blowjob on the Internet one afternoon, I noticed four deep lines that ran across my forehead. With every penis-thrust into my throat, the lines moved up and down—I was no longer able to pay attention to anything but the wrinkles. The next day, I made an appointment to get it fixed, and I was hooked. I couldn't believe I had gone all that time without Botox; what was I thinking? I could have been giving wrinkle-free, upside-down BJs all this time!

And then, it was the exercise addiction. I hired a trainer and quickly became addicted to working out; some mornings, I awoke at 4:00 a.m. so that I could hit the gym before going to a shoot. For years, I refused to travel out of state unless the hotel had a fitness room, and days off were unimaginable. Always justified by "It's better than being addicted to pretty much anything else," I never saw anything seriously wrong with my compulsive behavior. Over the years, I got fillers, lasers, peels, needles, everything short of surgery to keep myself looking as young and thin as possible. Boyfriends would come and go, shaking their heads each time I shelled out hundreds, sometimes thousands of dollars for some new and revolutionary procedure, as girlfriends eagerly joined in on the fun/torture, enabling each other in the never-ending obsession to better ourselves.

"It's only because I'm on camera," I convinced myself.

"Okay honey, let me see my babies here." She was referring to the leeches. Elena walked into the room, and I opened my eyes. While the first two minutes had gone by painfully slowly, I was shocked to realize the twenty minutes was up. "Great! They look very, very full!"

I slowly looked down at my left arm, and saw that the leeches had doubled in size. As she peeled them off and put them into a jar, blood poured out of the holes they left. "Very good blood you have, you won't bleed for more than twenty-four hours," she smiled. Twenty-four hours sounded like a long time, but what did I know? Blood quickly pooled on the massage table under me, which she cleaned up with paper towels. The amount of blood scared me—she saw the fear on my face, and assured me: "This is normal, it mean you have healthy blood." She escorted me out of her house wrapped in cotton balls and plastic wrap, but not before showing me pictures of something called a "Cleopatra facial," which entailed placing leeches on my liver, then forcing them to vomit my collected blood, and proceeding to use that blood as a mask on my face. I smiled politely, falsely promising I would consider it, and drove home looking like a modern-day makeshift mummy. Somehow, I had also let her convince me to take the "babies" home—informing me that, otherwise, she'd just have to get rid of them—so I rode home with the leeches, the ones full of my blood, in a plastic iced-coffee cup. By the time I walked into my house, the cotton balls on my arms had turned red and blood was piling up in the creases of the plastic wrap. I entered the living room where Toni was watching a movie, looking like I had gotten surgery in some shady basement (not far from the truth).

Toni looked up from the television, his smile quickly fading upon seeing me. "What are you up to now?"

"I have to go take care of this, I'll be right out to explain," I said as I quickly walked past him.

"What's in the cup?" I heard him yell as I entered my bathroom.

"I'll explain later!" I yelled back.

I replaced the cotton balls with some gauze, and brought the leeches into the kitchen. I wondered if it was bad that I was wrapping myself in gauze after she, the professional, had sent me home in plastic wrap. As I looked for something more suitable than a plastic cup for the babies, Toni walked in. "So, are you going to tell me what you're doing?"

I looked at him out of the side of my eye and saw that he did not look happy. "I'm looking for a jar to put my leeches in."

Toni put his face up to the plastic cup. "Euwwwwww." He scrunched up his nose. "What are these for? Let me guess. To make you look younger?"

"I have to shoot in two days, and I still have bruises on my arms from the cool sculpt—I heard about this method so I went to the doctor to get the blood sucked from my bruise today." Doctor. It was sort of true.

"You mean, the leeches are going to suck the blood?"

"No, they already did."

"Are you supposed to do it again on yourself?"

"No." I found a jar. "It's done. How was your shoot today?"

"It was good, we had to change location, but after that it was smooth. Why did you bring them home?"

"She was gonna kill them otherwise. Why did you have to change location?"

"Marianne double-booked, so she's going to give us a free day at her house next week. What are you going to do with these worms?"

"I think I'm just gonna keep them alive. She said if I wanted to bring them back next time, it would be cheaper than getting her to use new leeches. So are you gonna use her house for the anal scene?"

"Who?"

"Marianne. For location." I grabbed a leech with my fingers from the plastic cup to transfer to the Mason jar.

"No, I mean who are you bringing the leeches back to?"

"The lady who did the whole thing, she's like a holistic healer or something."

"I thought you said it was a doctor."

"I mean she's sort of a doctor but just like…an alternative medicine one."

Toni watched warily as I struggled to get the leeches to stay in the jar. "You need to stop doing all this. You are approaching dangerous territory." He said the last part extra slowly.

I shrugged and took the leeches to my bedroom.

The next morning, I went straight to the bathroom mirror after waking up. Unbelievably, my bruises were almost completely gone! I ran to the kitchen, where Toni was already up having coffee. "Look!" I threw my arms up. "The bruising has almost all disappeared!"

Toni looked closely and could not deny the results. "I have to say, Ashka, it looks really good."

"Okay so now that it worked, I have to tell you how fucking weird this place was." I told Toni all about Elena, the basement, the hocus-pocus she made me say out loud as she shook my legs. "I don't know, I'm not expecting anything for the nipple though.

I mean it was only sixty dollars, and I was already there," I defended myself.

"Well how does your nipple look now?" Toni asked.

"I don't know, I haven't...," I pulled down my shirt, and to my amazement, my nipple was completely clear of any irritation. A state I had not seen it in for nearly a year. "Holy fucking shit." Toni's eyes widened. "So it worked."

I was in disbelief. "I feel like fucking crying. You don't understand how weird that place was! I can't fucking believe this," I started to laugh. "I feel like I'm dreaming."

My nipple was healed, my bruises would likely be gone by the time I was shooting my gangbang, *and* I had proved Toni wrong—this was turning out to be an exceptional experience.

Later that day, I made an appointment for the Cleopatra facial.

HAIKU

Serial killing
Definition: must hit three
Just like a gangbang

The Prank

Mercury was in retrograde, which would be the worst time for a team-building weekend in Big Bear. Dave had rented a ranch for the entire summer to record an album with his band Mangchi, and he had invited the cast of the podcast up. The plan was to hang out, just relax, take some photos for our Instagram accounts, and, of course, record some episodes.

"I don't know if this is a good idea," I told Dave. "Mercury is in retrograde."

Dave laughed. "You and that shit. Just come."

"But it's not good to travel when…"

"Just come, it'll be fun."

So we all went.

DVDASA had been going on for two years now. Although we preferred to call it a "show," it was a podcast that my most famous friend David Choe and I had started after years of talking about wanting our own radio show. The letters stood for double vag, double anal, sensitive artist, but we told people it was short for David Asa. It had gained somewhat of a cult following and had even hit number one on the iTunes charts a couple of times. We recorded episodes every Tuesday with a group of Dave's employees, none of whom wanted to be there. Dave and I were similar in many ways, one being that we both had a compulsion to share every thought with the world, the worse the thought, the better. Known to some as the "Facebook Artist," Dave was a graffiti-artist-turned-fine-artist who was a legitimate millionaire. For this reason, we never had to worry about sponsors or making the show a lucrative endeavor—in fact, it only *cost* money; we used the show as our weekly social gathering, unfiltered and unedited. Each episode was supposed to be an hour and a half, but we were rarely able to keep it under three hours. We also tried to refrain from talking about anal sex every episode, and we always failed. As a podcast fan, I had to admit, our unorganized, irreverent, tasteless show was one that I would never listen to— but recording it was my favorite part of the week. The show was ninety percent of my social life; the other ten percent was in New York City, where I was returning to less and less, and Spiegler.

It's impossible to tell a *DVDASA* story without describing each cast member. So here is a brief bio of each of them, based on how they'd be if they were my husband:

BOBBY TRIVIA

Bobby is probably the most husband material out of all of the guys. As we often say, Bobby is the purest one of us all—he believes in things like true love and equal-effort sixty-nine-ing. He's Dave's money guy, which proves his trustworthiness—I mean I doubt it gets any more reliable than being an accountant in general. He could do my taxes every year, which would be amazing, because it's always been my dream to just blow someone and have that magically taken care of. And how fucking great would it be to end every night with a round of trivia? The loser would have to be on top the next time we fuck. His skin is naturally this dark golden hue, which is actually my tanning-color goal—so that would be great if we made babies. Speaking of which—I truly believe Bobby would make a great dad. He's funny, he's patient, he's kind, he's a lot like my own father, and he actually looks a little bit like him too. That part could be weird.

MONEY MARK

Money Mark is someone with equal amounts of pros and cons, marriage-wise. On one hand, he is the only real grownup on our show, he is the ideal age for me, he is an amazing cook, he is funny, he doesn't air his dirty laundry on the show like the rest of us, and oh yeah, he is a musical genius. He has kids, which would normally be on the con side of the list, but his kids are fucking awesome. Plus, they're pretty much grown, so it's not like he has to go to PTA meetings with his baby momma or anything. BUT—as a musician, he is always on the road, which is something I don't think I could handle. This one thing is such a deal-breaker for me that it is as important as all of the good things I mentioned about him combined. Even though I crave my own space and freedom like it's my energy source, I'm also extremely needy (I'm the worst, I know) and couldn't handle that much distance.

CRITTER

Critter is the kind of guy who, in an apocalyptic situation, you could trust to take care of everything while you took a nap in the panic room. Or if a *Taken*-esque kidnapping were to happen, he would totally be a great Liam Neeson and not give up on finding me, ever. He's a gentleman in the true sense of the word and has the best manners of all the guys on the show. While he's sort of quiet on the show, real-life Critter is full of good stories and very funny. He has a quality about him that makes him impossible not to like. Physically, Critter is a universally perfect specimen—blonde with light eyes, tall, and sturdily built. His aspirations, though, don't fit with mine: While I'm hoping to retire in a penthouse suite of a hotel and spend my old age on heroin, writing, and getting fat, Critter wants to live on a huge ranch (ugh, nature) engaging in torturous activities like fishing and getting drunk.

VAL

Val would be the worst to be married to, and not just because he has hit a woman because she was annoying him at CPK. He would definitely, one hundred percent cheat on me—and not in an open-relationship kind of way, but in a he-has-a-secret-Tinder-account kind of way. He once cat-fished a woman into flying across the country to come live with him, all the while telling her his name was Aaron. Come to think of it, do we even know if Val is his real name? He is a dangerous man.

DAVE

Dave is kind of the best man for me—if things were completely different. His personality is perfect. He is funny, intelligent, and relentlessly curious. When he gives the BFE (boyfriend experience), it's magical: He is loving, attentive, and so much fun. At the same time, he is just as selfish as me, and he has so much going on that he's not the kind of guy I'd feel like his happiness depended on my actions. I imagine ours would be the kind of relationship where we do our own shit during the day and then come together at night. Maybe I'm totally wrong. I've had sex with him before, so I know he's good at it. I'd never be bored with him, because he likes to talk even more than I do. Also, I can't decide whether I like Fat Dave or (relatively) Skinny Dave better—both are equally attractive in their own ways. His sense of style is probably the best on the show (homeless chic.) He is someone whose character judgments I can completely respect—just look at the people around him. When he says someone is horrible (which is often), I generally agree wholeheartedly. I also think I could (pretty easily) convince him into a three-way with a transsexual hooker. On the down side, he's a sensitive artist and has totally fucked-up views on long-term relationships. He's self-destructive. Also, Dave shits his pants suspiciously often for a full-grown adult—which I think is sort of a metaphor for his entire being.

But back to Big Bear and the team-building weekend: It was noon and we had all been awake for a couple of hours. Having stayed up late the previous night arguing about which was more gay (sucking dick or French kissing), conversation this morning had been kept to the bare minimum of "I made coffee" and "Thanks." I was lying on the sofa, catching up on all of my social media feeds on my phone, when a text from Dave came in.

`Wanna play a prank on everyone?`

Because we are the same person, I knew where he was going with this. The previous night, Dave and I had slept in the same room. The ranch had enough rooms for everyone, but most were detached from the main house—in order to get to them, one had to walk outside, in the dark, up some creaking stairs, into separate cottages. The rooms in the main house were all already occupied by Mangchi members, and even though I was scared of the dark, even though I had never lived in a house, and even though I was *the only girl there* (I pulled this card only when desperate), no one wanted to trade with me—so Dave offered me his bed, and he slept on the sofa in the master suite. This is the kind of millionaire Dave is.

`Let's tell everyone we fucked!` I wrote back, making sure no one was close enough to me to see my phone.

`I'm in Bobby's room, I already told him. He's so excited,` he replied.

I should note here that Dave and I had sex when we first met.

It had been a few years since I'd been in porn, and I'd been cast as the lead in a movie called *PURE* for the late David Aaron Clarke. It was my first big role, and I considered it to be my big break. Yoshi, an editor at the production company shooting *PURE*, knew that Dave was a fan of mine. He made the introduction, inviting Dave to the set. We exchanged numbers, and a few days later, we hung out and realized we were the same person. In a heated moment while watching *The Human Centipede* at my house, we had sex. We continued as fuck buddies, lost touch, became fuck buddies again, lost touch again, and became fuck buddies again. We did this a few times before the whole Facebook thing happened, he went off to rehab, and I married Toni. People often ask me why Dave and I never progressed past fuck buddies; I blame this entirely on Dave. He was (and continues to be) anti-relationship. I think when he meets the right girl, he could be an amazing boyfriend.

I went back up to the master bedroom and texted Dave again.

`Lemme know when you wanna record, I'm going back upstairs to get some writing done.`

A few hours later, a group message came through to my phone from Dave's manager saying that they were ready to start the show. We all met in the living room, where Bobby was smiling like an excited child. He was sitting next to Dave, and when I walked by, he looked at me.

"Oh, are you sitting there?" I asked awkwardly.

"No, you sit next to Dave," Bobby got up.

I gave Bobby a "don't be weird" look and sat on the sofa across from them.

What proceeded was an hour of Dave and me lying.

"We dry-humped."

"Okay, well, we may as well say it then—we had sex."

"I came inside of her."

"What? I thought you said you didn't."

"I told her to call me Toni."

"No comment."

At the end of the episode, we revealed that we had been playing a joke on everyone; we read the text messages from earlier that morning, everyone had a good laugh, and we went on a hike and complained the entire time that we were on a hike. When the episode aired, Dave and I watched the comments roll in giddily— would people fall for it? Would they be just as excited as the rest of the cast had been when we revealed it was all a joke?

The answers were yes and no. Everyone did fall for it. The problem was, half the people didn't listen until the end, so they just continued on with their lives believing it to be a true story. The other half thought we were just lying about lying, and assumed that we really had fucked.

To this day, I'm asked at least once a week whether or not I was unfaithful to Toni, whether Dave and I really did fuck in Big Bear, and whether or not we are currently engaging in an affair. It's a tired subject, and it's become one of those things where I'm telling the truth, but feel the guilt of being dishonest. Nobody seems to believe me, and I wonder sometimes if the fun of the prank was worth being labeled a liar.

The answer is probably yes. But I should have known; Mercury in retrograde was not a good time for a prank.

HAIKU

Dropped a blueberry
Under the oven it rolls
Goodbye, forever

A Bad Day

I was supposed to fuck my husband that day. To be more precise, I was supposed to fuck my husband that day for money.

It was the first day on the set for my new showcase movie, title yet to be determined. I had shot numerous showcase movies before, but this one was different, because months prior, we had put out a call on social media:

Thinking of doing a "fan request" movie... Is there anything you've been dying to see me do? Types of scenes/outfits/girls/guys?

It was not a groundbreaking idea; reaching out to fans for requests was something that had been done many times before. But it was my first time. Answers started to come in right away, and by the end of the day, it was clear what the frontrunners were: hardcore anal, black guys, blowbang, lesbian scene with Kendra Lust, Harajuku Girl outfit, double penetration. ("Fuck me" and "Shut up and show me your asshole" were popular answers as well, but we decided not to go with them.)

For my hardcore anal scene, I chose my husband Toni to work

with. Upon hearing this, one might think I took the easy route—what could be less work than fucking my own husband? But one would be mistaken. When I worked with Toni, I was his ragdoll. He was the one I could submit to best: no holes barred. Toni is insane when the camera is rolling—by the time the director yells "cut," I am so sore that I need to rest for an hour before I can drive myself home. A scene with him guaranteed me three sore holes, multiple bruises, and a genuine feeling of "What the fuck just happened; why was there a foot in my vagina?"

And I liked it.

That's not to say our home sex was like this. Off camera, we fucked like any other normal couple: For two minutes, in the missionary position, ending in a cream pie where I ran off to pee his cum out before either of us could say "married sex." Porn sex, for both of us, was our fantasy sex. It was the dirty secret you couldn't tell your wife. Except instead of a secret, it was packaged and sold for the whole world to see on their TVs and computer screens.

The day started off like any other shoot day. I woke up at 6:00 a.m., just as the sun was rising, to clean my asshole. What this entailed was me filling up an enema bag with a gallon of water, releasing the water through a tube into my anus, letting the water out, repeating for an hour, or until the water came out clear, whichever happened first. It was disgusting, it was unattractive, but that's what it took for an anal scene to be masturbation-worthy, unless, of course, you were making scat porn, which I have not. But no judging.

Somewhere around round three of filling up the enema bag, I noticed a commotion outside my bathroom. Above my bathtub is a giant frosted window my full height in both length and width, and on the other side is our backyard. The window is frosted enough that you can't see anything, but it's clear enough that you can tell when something is moving outside. I texted Toni.

Are you smoking in the backyard?
He replied right away, Yes.
Can you not, right now? I'm cleaning out so you
can buttfuck me later.
Toni and I are not morning people. For this reason, along
with the fact that I crave my own space, Toni and I have separate
bedrooms, separate bathrooms, and separate offices. We don't see
each other in the morning until we both venture into the common
areas of our home, when we are both ready to start the day. We
had not yet initiated conversation that day, and this was not a
good way to do so.
I can't even see you, he texted.
I can see you moving and it's making me too shy
to enema. Please, I replied.
Where the fuck am I supposed to smoke?
I don't give a fuck. I'm on a tight schedule.
Just please.
I could hear Toni getting up and swearing in Spanish. I knew
he was swearing because swear words were the only ones I understood in his native tongue. He slammed the door, and I sighed in
relief. I felt bad to kick him out of a common area and to start
his day like this—but he was crazy to think I was comfortable
cleaning my insides out into a toilet while I could practically hear
him inhaling his cigarette. I would apologize later when there
wasn't a plastic tube in my asshole.
I spent the next hour on the toilet in a horrible mood. It was
hard to get clean that morning, which sometimes happens, and I
was running late—so I rushed out of the house without apologizing
to Toni. I texted him once I was on the set in the makeup chair.
I'm sorry. I was in a rush, and you being RIGHT
THERE wasn't helping.
He didn't respond. I texted him again when we started on my
hair, this time using a term of endearment.

`I'm sorry Papo...I love u.`

Again, no response. Did I anger him that much? I didn't think my behavior was worthy of ignoring me...especially on a day when we were working together. Was he mad at me for something else? Had I done something earlier, maybe last night? I tried to come up with something, but I couldn't.

I wiggled around in the makeup chair, unable to get comfortable. Usually, I excelled at sitting still while my face and hair were done—makeup artists regularly complimented me on my ability to stay still. I attributed this to my yoga practice. "They teach us that if you can control your breath, you can control anything," I would proudly boast. But today, between the thought of Toni being mad at me and the fact that it had been hard to clean my asshole out, my anxiety would not let me be a stoic yogi. What if I wasn't completely clean? What if it got messy during the scene? What if I shit on my already-mad husband? I apologized to Lena, the makeup artist. "I'm having a weird day," I explained.

Before Toni was to arrive, the plan was to shoot a solo masturbation scene in my Harajuku Girl outfit. The wardrobe girl had put together an outfit with about nine hundred layers, complete with a rainbow tutu and ribbons in my pigtails. I looked in the mirror and thought I might be the oldest woman in the world at this moment wearing her hair like this. The colorful outfit did not reflect how I felt on the inside. I felt like a fucking clown: depressed and wearing the mask of a laughing face.

I sighed and sent Toni one last text before throwing my phone in my purse.

`Why u ignore me? :(`

"Okay, here are the toys. They're all washed, I'll leave them here on the table, and you can just choose whatever your heart desires once we're rolling. We don't need you to use all of them, but just do you, and we'll capture it." Jonathan was the director. As he said, he had laid out ten or so sex toys, all different colors, shapes, and textures. Most of them were pretty standard—vibrators, dildoes, buttplugs. But there in the center, were two ping-pong-sized glass marbles. I picked them up and looked at Jonathan. He shrugged, raising his eyebrows. Was he challenging me?

We shot a striptease for an hour, where I drove the crew crazy by playing the same Katy Perry song over and over the entire time. "I want to make sure I stay on the same tempo!" I claimed, but in truth, I just loved the song. And the fact that everyone hated it somehow pleased me more.

Once the tease was shot, the music was turned off and the crew quieted down.

"Alright, are we ready to do this sonofabitch?" Jonathan asked the room. Everyone nodded. "Let's do this shit."

"Don't say 'shit' on an anal day!" I panicked.

"Sorry, sorry I forgot. Alright everyone: No saying the S word on an anal day! Alright, let's do this! Slate..." I clapped my hands, "...and action!"

"Do you wanna watch me fuck myself?" I asked the camera lens in a voice at least two octaves higher than my real voice. I drooled, letting my saliva drip down to my pussy, at which point I started to fuck myself with my hand.

Masturbating on camera is a lot different from masturbating in real life. Much like sex with Toni, the porn version lasted much longer. At home, it took me thirty seconds to get off; I'd squeeze my eyes shut, my face and body both contorting into weird shapes that I'd literally rather die than let the world see. Yet I always came harder when there was a camera on me. Maybe because I took my time, pacing myself, building an orgasm up for longer than half a minute—or maybe because people were watching, and I am an attention whore.

I went through every dildo, vibrator, and buttplug, came with each one, and was relieved that my ass juices were completely clear and free of color. If I could go through all of this without getting messy, the anal scene later was guaranteed to be clean as well. I looked down at the table beside me and saw that the only items left were the glass marbles. I had decided earlier these would be my finale. One by one, I put them in my asshole. I took a dildo I had used earlier and started to fuck myself. The plan was to fuck myself and let the marbles fall out as I did so. Whenever I orgasmed, my pussy and ass would contract, and I figured this would force the marbles out.

I fucked myself for about two minutes before I felt an orgasm building up. "Here we go," I thought, as I came, the insides of my two holes throbbing. I felt a marble come out, and for a moment wondered if this is what orgasmic birth felt like. *Well I'll definitely be doing THIS again*, I thought as I continued to fuck myself post-orgasm, waiting for the second marble to drop.

Five Minutes Later...

The fucking second marble had not yet made an appearance. I put my middle finger in my asshole to see exactly where it was, and to my horror, it felt like any other time I fingered my rectum, just flesh, no marble.

"Hang on guys," I looked past the camera. "I can't find it."

"Okay, let's take five," Jonathan yelled.

I ran to the bathroom, grabbing my purse on the way to check if Toni had replied.

He hadn't.

Thirty Minutes Later...

The fucking piece-of-S-word marble was nowhere to be seen.

"Are you sure it didn't come out and you didn't notice?" Jonathan asked.

"Yes Jonathan, I am sure."

"Are we sure no one saw the marble come out of Asa's butt while she was fucking herself?" Jonathan yelled across room. "Anyone?"

Everyone shook their head, as I hung my own down in embarrassment.

"Alright then," Jonathan sighed, "Let's just break for lunch. Honey, just try to relax for a few. You're probably tensing up, and I'm sure that's not helping."

I hated when people called me Honey. For a moment, I hoped the marble would never come out so I could just go home and eat pizza.

I grabbed my phone and laid down on the sofa.

"You okay?" Lena asked.

"Yeah. Today is just really weird. I think I just need to not think about this marble right now."

"Yeah, a watched pot doesn't boil. Come here, I'll touch you up."

I sat back into the makeup chair, and felt a pang of guilt and self-hatred. I had already been in this situation before—a few years back, I was shooting a lesbian anal scene where we stuffed each other with Chinese harmony balls. The cool thing about them is that once they're inside of you, they click against each other and the little bells in them ring whenever you move. As we started the scene, Annie had joked "I hope they don't get stuck!" and ten minutes later, that was exactly what happened. The director had seen this happen before and calmly told me to just take a break and gravity would do its job. He was right.

The fact that this was my second time with some kind of ball stuck inside of me was too shameful for me to reveal to anyone on the set. It was kind of like having two abortions: First time, shame on Chinese harmony ball; second time, shame on me.

It was turning out to be one of those days when nothing was

going right, and why even bother trying, because everything was just going to go wrong anyway. I felt like crying, but instead I closed my eyes and held back my tears, for fear of humiliating myself further.

"My friend's actually a nurse in the ER," Lena said as she reapplied the foundation I had drooled off of my chin. "She always tells me about the crazy things people show up with stuck in their butts. One time, a guy showed up a with a Fiji bottle stuck in there."

"Does she think the Richard Gere thing is true?" I asked.

"I asked her the same thing. She says she's actually never seen anyone come in with a gerbil in their ass."

"Maybe people got scared after hearing about Richard Gere."

"I don't know, maybe. One time, I was fucking this guy..."

Just then, my phone went off. It was a message from Toni.

Sorry, I was in the gym. Don't worry, my love! Driving to you now, do you need anything?

And, right on cue, I felt my whole body exhale as if a Valium had just kicked in.

"Hang on," I interrupted Lena, and ran to the bathroom. I stuck my middle finger in my asshole.

There it was, the marble. I pushed, once again thinking of orgasmic births, and walked out onto the set.

"It's out!" I yelled.

"Alright then," Jonathan cheered. "Let's finish this sonofabitch!"

We wrapped up the masturbation scene just as Toni arrived, and my whole mood changed—it was as if the day had started over again.

Toni threw me down onto the sofa, and I spread my legs wide. "I want you in my ass," I begged him. "Please, take my ass." It was about ten minutes into the sex scene.

Toni fucked my pussy again, and right as I was about to cum, he pulled his cock and rubbed it on my asshole. What a fucking tease. He knew this drove me crazy—he knew it would make me beg for it even more.

I rubbed my clit, begging him to continue, as he slowly pushed his cock into my most popular hole. As I loosened up, he fucked me harder and harder, until finally he was just pounding the S-word out of me. I came hard, my holes tightening up once again, and just when I felt my heart couldn't beat any faster, it started to slow down. Both my pussy and ass pulsed, and I smiled, looking up at Toni while my senses came back to me. I tried to catch my breath through my mouth—I always did this thing when I came, when I would hold my breath for the entire orgasm—sometimes it made me feel like I was going to faint afterward. Just then, I felt a sharp pain on my ass cheek. As my body normalized, the pain became sharper—I looked down to see if we were fucking on a piece of broken glass.

ARE YOU FUCKING KIDDING ME?!?!?!

"Holy fuck, a bee stung me!" I said in a voice at least two octaves lower than normal.

Toni stopped fucking me, and as the cameramen came out from behind their viewfinders, I plucked the bee out of my cheek and threw it on the table next to me. "What a little asshole!"

Toni's demeanor changed immediately, from sexy lover to concerned husband. "Are you okay? You're not allergic, are you?"

"I don't know," I answered, still out of breath. "I've never been stung."

"Do you wanna take a break?" Toni asked.

I shook my head no. "Let's just keep fucking." I turned to the cameramen. "If my face starts swelling up, just let me know."

"Are you sure, we can..." I could tell Jonathan didn't know what to do.

"I promise, I'm fine. I don't wanna lose momentum." I couldn't fucking believe what had just happened. Could this day be any worse? Why was this happening to me?

We continued on to complete what I believe to be one of my best scenes of all time. Of course, Toni came in my eye, breaking a run of two years without pinkeye, because how else could a workday like that end?

Driving home, I told Toni about what had happened earlier— how I had trouble cleaning my ass, how a marble got stuck, how I was worried he was mad at me, and how as soon as he texted me, the marble came out. I started to cry, feeling I had just gone through a day where the whole world was against me. *Feel sorry for meeee*, I projected with my sobs, hoping he would answer with something like *let's just go home, pick a movie you like, any movie, and order some pizza.*

"Are you about to get your menstruation?" Toni calmly asked.

I stopped crying, and my mouth opened wide in shock. Normally I laughed when he referred to my period as *menstruation*, but all I was hearing was *everything you just said is invalid because you're emotional due to your crazy female hormones.*

"...Are you fucking kidding me right now?"

"It sounds like you're about to get your *tomatito*," he smiled.

Did this motherfucker think I was going to laugh? Did he think he was being funny? "Don't even talk to me right now," I said in my most serious voice, and turned my body to face the window. What men don't understand is that the reason asking us if we are on our period is so fucked up is not because we are offended that they think we are bleeding out of our vaginas. It's not even because they think we are bitches once a month. It's because by asking us if we are PMSing, they take all the justification out of why we are *really* upset. With his question, Toni had just revealed that he thought everything that happened to me wasn't as big of a deal as I had thought, that I was overreacting, that I shouldn't be as upset as I was.

We got home and I went straight to my room. I took my dinner alone (a salad, yuck!) and went to sleep early without saying good night.

The next morning when I went to pee, there was blood on my underwear.

I didn't tell Toni.

Haiku

Fuck you, kale salad
You're not a real fucking meal
I'm still hungry, dick

On Womanhood

If I woke up tomorrow as a man, the first thing I would do is find someone to fuck me in my ass. I've known this for a while now. Certainly every woman has given this some thought before, at least once in her lifetime—not anal sex (although probably that too), but the idea of waking up one morning as a member of the opposite sex. As one can easily see from a quick Google search, I love anal play. But I'll bet anal play with a prostate would be even better.

After my first prostate-induced orgasm (and probably my last for at least a few hours, because I'm pretty sure that's how the male anatomy works), I would spend the rest of my day the way I normally do, regardless of my new gender. I'd run errands, go to work, get home, and watch some bad reality shows I had recorded. I suppose I'd take advantage of my faster metabolism and eat a large pizza. And then I'd go to bed, hoping to wake up back in my female body.

The thing is, I love being a woman. I love my body, I love the clothing I get to wear, I love the emotions I feel, I love the friendships I have, I love having three holes to be penetrated in, I love peeing in a seated position. Sure, it would be fun to be a man for a little while and see how the other half lives—but really, five minutes (long enough to see what their orgasms are like) would be enough. The only thing I can honestly say I'm envious of is men's ability to be promiscuous without judgment.

I often wonder if I would have picked the same profession if I were a man. As a woman with a high sex drive, porn is the perfect job—it's a way I can celebrate my sexuality, a way for me to use it to my advantage. I figure, if the world is going to judge me for indulging in my horniness anyway, why not make money doing it? If I were a man, though, being hypersexual would just be seen as normal. "He's a dude, of course he's going to get laid every chance he gets," people would think when I had casual sex. Don't get me wrong, I'm happy with my decision to be in porn, and if I could live my life over, I would make the same decision. But it's hard not to think "What if?"

Why is it the norm for men to have all the sex they want, but not us? Why is it that when we go out looking for sex, we are described as "acting like men"? If we aren't meant to enjoy sex, why does it feel so good? Why are we born with clitorises if they are not meant to be stimulated?

The older I get, the more I decide I'm done with that bullshit. When I'm being sexual, I'm being me—I'm being a woman. Fuck apologizing. Fuck making excuses. I'll fuck when I want.

Toni and I met as performers on a porn set, in what ended up being my first double-penetration scene. That means that on our first encounter, there was another man's penis in my vagina as he fucked my asshole. This was within fifteen minutes of saying "Nice to meet you."

Now, I don't believe in love at first sight. However, I do believe some people have such strong sexual chemistry that after fucking for the first time, even if you know absolutely nothing else about them, you want to fuck them again and again for the rest of your life. This is how I felt when I met Toni. I asked him for his number, eventually did end up falling in love, and three years later, we got married.

Toni has been in porn for over twenty years. I always joke to him that that's longer than I've been giving blowjobs. He's been at it since he was nineteen years old. I wonder if I will be in it for that long. The answer is, probably not—I've been in it for seven years, in another thirteen, I'll be forty-three, which in porn star years for a woman is like being a great-great-great-grandmother. For women, time in porn goes by in something like dog years: seven times the rate of a man.

Within the industry, I'd say the life of a female porn star is much more glamorous than that of our male counterparts. We have more say in who we do and what we do, we get at least triple the camera time, and we get up to five times the pay. We are treated as stars on the set, while the men are treated more like props. We can demand things like fresh Hawaiian papaya and vegan cupcakes, while the men are lucky to get bottled water.

Outside of the industry, however, it is a different story. As women, we are labeled "whores," while the men are just considered overall awesome. The men *get to fuck* every day; the women *get fucked* every day. It's dumb, but that's the way most people look at it. As if the sentence "She gets to fuck guys every day" doesn't even make sense.

For this, I'm extremely jealous of Toni. Sometimes, I let him know.

"Has being a man slut ever even affected your life in a negative way?" I asked him once.

He laughed. He didn't even need to give an answer.

"No really, think about it—has your sexuality ever gotten you into a bad situation? Or where people judged you for it?"

He thought about it, and I could tell he was doing so really hard because he actually paused his video game. "I got caught jerking off in the lobby of my neighbor's building when I was thirteen."

By his smile, I could tell this wasn't a traumatic experience. "What happened?"

"The neighbor told my parents. I forgot about it until now."

"And that's it?"

His video game was still on pause. He thought about it for a bit. "That's it."

"And everyone who finds out you're in porn just thinks you're like hot shit, right?"

He laughed. "Of course."

See? I really didn't even need to ask.

Toni and I aren't swingers. While it doesn't upset him that I fuck other guys for a living, it doesn't turn him on to hear about it either. We aren't the kind of couple that tells each other the details of our sex scenes with others at the end of the day, followed by a blowjob where he grunts "Yeah, tell me you liked sucking that other guy's dick" before he cums all over my face. I've been in those relationships before, and while they can be fun, that's just not what Toni and I have.

When I asked him if he'd prefer to be married to a non-slut, my husband immediately without thinking answered, "Of course not. Then it wouldn't be you."

I pressed on. "No, really, though—what if I were exactly the same, except I had only fucked like...five guys before I met you? And I was a doctor instead of a porn star?"

He answered quickly again. "It doesn't really make a difference. It's not like it changes the way you are with me."

I believed him when he said this, and I continue to believe him. In the five years since I met him, he has never once used the term "slut" in a negative way. Not even during our worst fights has he ever thrown my sexuality in my face. The truth is, I think, he just genuinely doesn't see it as a bad thing—it's just a part of who I am, nothing more. This is my first relationship like this.

I wish a partner like this upon every slut out there.

In this chapter are three stories in which I felt I was a woman in a man's world. In sharing them, I hope to share the lesson I learned: that what I felt was false.

It's a fucking woman's world too.

SLUT

"The reason Jimmy dumped you is because he thought you were a slut. He wanted to fix you, but he says you're a lost cause."

It was the first time I had ever been called that, "slut."

I was in the fifth grade.

I didn't even know what the word meant. That night, I looked it up in the dictionary.

Slut /slet/
noun
A woman with low standards of cleanliness.

I was confused.

My room was clean. My clothes were freshly washed, and I showered every morning before school. What about me was dirty?

It would be another year before I knew the full meaning of the word, and a few more after that before dictionaries were updated to include the (now) more common definition:

Slut /slet/
noun
A woman considered sexually promiscuous.

Even then, I didn't know what Jimmy meant. At the time of his accusation, Jimmy was the only boy I had kissed. It was once, on a dare from his best friend in a game of "truth or dare" on a school field trip. It was hardly scandalous—it wasn't even French.

Looking back, I realize that Jimmy didn't know the meaning of the word either—it makes me wonder what had given this eleven-year-old boy the premonition, if that's what it was. Did he just have a sixth sense that I'd grow up to love sex? We barely knew what sex was, let alone that having a lot of it was considered a negative thing. Who or what had put that word in his mouth? Or maybe the word implied more than just sleeping around. Maybe the word represented feminine sexuality as a whole. As a young girl just starting to bleed for the first time, not only was my body starting to change, my personality was becoming more feminine too. At the same time my breasts had started to grow, my girlfriends and I were getting becoming more social, and we were now ditching playing games for gossiping about boys during recess, shopping at the mall on weekends for clothes, and wearing lots of lip gloss. I was most definitely a "girly girl" and quickly becoming a sexual being and attracting male attention, something perfectly natural, so much so that it's practically animalistic. Without knowing the exact definition, it was enough for young Jimmy to recognize this behavior as *slutty*, which is really, really sad.

The next time someone called me a slut was in the ninth grade, the year I lost my virginity, the year I fucked sixteen guys before summer vacation. Over the years since my first kiss, it became gradually apparent that I was more sexually driven than other girls my age; I was the first to get fingered, first to give a handjob, first to give a blowjob, and eventually, first to fuck. As I grew more sexual, so did my fondness for the word; when I first found out that people in my school were calling me a "slut," I distinctly remember feeling flattered. *Me?* I bashfully thought. *Why, thank you.* When girls talked shit behind my back, I felt above them; they were just as boy-crazy as I was, and I was doing something they were all afraid to do. When boys called me a slut, I smiled; it felt like a compliment. I took my peers' comments and interpreted them as *you are cool, you are so fucking cool.*

It wasn't until I fell in love that I realized I had romanticized a term that others had meant as a snub.

"It's hard for me to defend you, when you were such a slut before me," Kevin would often say to me. We were fifteen, and when I met him, my world changed. He was a virgin, and I was not, not even close. My existence became something solely for him—I suddenly couldn't fathom life without him. I ditched school to be with him, I stole from stores to give him presents, I snuck out of my house at 2:00 a.m. to spend the night with him. If killing every boy I had fucked meant getting my virginity back, I would have done it—it was the one thing he wanted from me that I couldn't give. It caused countless arguments over the four years we dated. "You're such a *slut*," he would growl, putting an emphasis on the last word like it disgusted him to even voice such a thing. "You let those guys just use you. I *love* you."

I would cry.

After Kevin and I broke up, I went back to sleeping with whomever I pleased, in abundance, until a twenty-seven-year-old Puerto Rican sports bookie named Eddie swept me off my feet a few months later. He loved that I was sexual, he loved that I was young. He loved hearing about the boys I had been with before, and he loved that he was my first *man*. When he called me a slut, he meant it the way I had originally perceived it: as a compliment. We quickly got married, and I entered my first open relationship. Sometimes telling each other, sometimes not, we each fucked people outside of our marriage. I started a job at a dungeon as a dominatrix before graduating to stripping a year later. Eddie loved it, bragging to his friends that his wife was in the sex industry. Had it not been for the prescription painkiller habit we both developed in the time we were together, we may never have gotten divorced. Then again, maybe we wouldn't have stayed together as long. It's hard to say now—either way, I'm grateful to Eddie for giving me back what I had lost: my confidence as a slut.

HERMIE

I was six years old when I was able to look at a vagina that was not my own. Of course, I had seen other ones briefly in passing, my mother's especially; but this was the first time I *looked* at one, examined it, if you will. My cousin Maya and I were in the shower at my aunt's house, which was huge and fancy. It's important to mention here how huge and fancy it was, because it's the only way you'll believe that I was sitting on the floor, shower running around my legs, as Maya walked around with her Cabbage Patch doll. We were playing house, covered in soap and shampoo. It was one of those showers with nine shower heads coming out of the wall, enclosed in a glass space that turns into a steam room if you turn on one of its twelve settings.

"It's time to go to bed now," I commanded in my best motherly tone to Maya. She headed toward me and sat down, kissed her doll on the head before gently laying it on the wet floor, and finally laid her own naked body down for me to tuck her in. What ensued was something I would forever wish I could take back. If I opened my closet door right now and found a time machine inside, this is the moment I would return to. I'd keep my eyes focused on her face, her chest, the doll, anywhere but where they went that day.

As Maya closed her eyes, pretending to go to sleep, waiting for me to tuck her in, my eyes went to her vagina.

There it was, her perfect little pussy. *That's what it's supposed to look like?* I silently panicked. It didn't look like mine. I had pieces of skin hanging out all over the place, she did not. Her vagina looked like Barbie's, but with a slit in the middle. Mine looked like Barbie's, if someone had put a slit in it and then pulled the insides out.

From that day on, I looked at every vagina that came my way as closely as I could, which unfortunately was not very closely.

Gym class, swimming class, sleepovers...for the rest of my child-
hood, any time girls were getting naked, I was secretly looking at
their vaginas. It wasn't an easy task, since I didn't want to seem
like I was so *desperate* to see pussies (which I was). I did all of
this while I did my best to cover my own, which I came to believe
was disfigured.

It's okay, I would tell myself. *You'll just never get naked in
front of anyone.*

My fear got worse when I reached middle school and learned
what a hermaphrodite was.

So that's what the hanging skin is, I thought. *My balls.*

A few times, I thought of asking my parents if they knew—
but I didn't want them to feel bad about it, so I kept my mouth
shut. I searched on the Internet a few times for procedures to
get my situation fixed, but I never really got a straight answer.
Eventually, I just kind of forgot about the whole thing—when
Dan Siegel fingered me in the seventh grade and didn't seem to
notice anything weird, I felt confident I could go through life the
way I was.

Then came high school. From summer vacation to summer
vacation, I fucked sixteen boys in my freshman year, which was
about sixteen times the amount of guys any of my girlfriends had
fucked. In my diary, I wrote about every sexual experience I had,
careful not to leave anything out—over and over, I would read
these entries, masturbating and losing sleep. Getting fucked in
spread-eagle position for the first time, swallowing cum for the
first time, fucking a twenty-two-year-old drummer who said I
could move in with him if I ever ran away from home—I wrote
about it all. Not only until my mom found the diary, did it come to
a halt. "You invaded my privacy!" I yelled what I had heard white
teenage girls say so many times on television. "I feel so violated."

In addition to the boys, I had also lightly hooked up with
a handful of girls (nothing past dry third base, aka touching

vaginas through underwear), but I felt they didn't count toward the official body count. It's hard to pinpoint why—maybe it was a penetration thing. Or maybe it just meant I'm straight. Either way, as soon as I discovered sex, everything else had to go. My grades dropped—causing me to get kicked out of school. I forgot all about my aspirations to get good grades, go to college, be a writer—all I wanted to do was smoke weed, meet boys, and fuck them.

One day, on a rare occasion when I was actually present in school, we were taught in health class about hormones. The class was gender-specific, girls only during fourth period, boys during fifth.

"Testosterone is what makes guys such horndogs," our teacher said to a class of giggling girls. "It's the reason they think about sex so much."

For the first time in months, I was learning something useful. *I knew it*, I thought. *I'm totally half male. My testosterone is what makes me so horny.*

I really thought like this for a long time. Everyone seemed to agree that while it was acceptable for boys to be so-called horndogs, girls were supposed to be pure and virginal while waiting for the "one." Secretly, I blamed my sexual behavior on my high testosterone levels. Somewhere, I went back to thinking that my pussy lips were the result of an underdeveloped ballsack.

Damn you, testosterone, I thought. *Why me?*

It wasn't until I was in porn, and I was looking at vaginas at tongue distance from my face on a daily basis, that I realized my own was completely normal. There were girls with pussies like my cousin's; there were girls with pussies like mine; there were girls whose pussy lips were bigger than mine; there were girls whose pussy lips were totally lopsided (still normal). I even met a girl named Skin Diamond who could be my genital twin—her vagina looks exactly like mine, only darker.

I've also had my hormones tested, and it turns out my testosterone levels are exactly where they should be. Basically, I spent my entire adolescence worrying about something that wasn't even real. This kind of pisses me off. If someone had just pulled me aside to tell me what I know now—that girls can be horny too!—it would have brought me so much relief.

From such a young age, we are taught that male sexuality is okay to express and female sexuality is not. We go as far as to explain this using science. So much so, that I thought I was a hermaphrodite—there is no way this is healthy. Whether you're male or female, growing up learning this will fuck you up! A boy taught this way will learn to identify a woman displaying any kind of sexuality (even something as simple as a low-cut shirt) as "bad behavior," or even worse, "asking for it." A young girl taught to suppress her sexuality learns that there are parts of herself that she cannot express, that she cannot enjoy. Either way, we are both being taught that women are not equal to men—that women are not allowed the same luxuries as men when it comes to sex.

It would be cool if we could look back on this kind of thing in a few years and think "God, that was *so* 2016."

THREE-WAY

We had finished our last bag of coke, and while we all acted like this was no big deal, it was a big fucking deal. It was 6:00 a.m., the sun was coming up. The five of us sat in Jade's living room: me, Luca, Tom, Jade, and Jade's then-boyfriend. I wondered the same thing as every other time I had ever done coke: *Why? I don't even like this stuff.* It made me anxious and withdrawn, too nervous to speak for fear of saying something stupid. My friends, on the other hand, loved the drug, and seemed to be doing more and more of it lately, mostly on the weekends. Not that it mattered what day of the week it was; none of us had real jobs. We had all been potheads together through high school, and now that we had graduated, now that we had nothing better to do, other drugs were coming into play. Although I usually avoided it, once in a while I ended up joining in on the coke sessions simply because if there was one thing worse than a coke high, it was being the sober one in a group of people high on coke. The worst part of all was that once I started a drug I didn't even like in the first place, it was impossibly hard to stop for the rest of the night—which was why, at 6:00 a.m., with the sun coming up, it mattered that we had just done our last bag.

Jade's boyfriend stretched his arms up, faking a yawn. "Wanna go to bed?" he asked his girlfriend. Motherfucker. He was hiding another bag. But what was I gonna do? We were among friends. I wasn't gonna out the guy. I turned to Luca and Tom.

"What are you guys doing now?"

"Tom's staying with me while Bella's in Greece. Wanna come over? I got Oxys." Luca smiled.

Ah, finally. Some opiates. This was something I could get down with.

Bella was Luca's girlfriend, someone I had yet to meet, despite the fact they had been together for two years. She spent her summers in Greece, this much I knew—it seemed that was the only time any of us saw Luca anymore.

We said our awkward goodbyes, and I heard Jade whisper, "Where is it?" as soon as the door closed behind us. Already hot and humid at this early hour, I tried and failed to think of something worse than coming down from coke when the sun was coming up. Hardly speaking, the three of us got into a cab and rode in silence to Luca's apartment.

Luca's parents were rich, the richest among any of the kids in our group of friends. It had been over a year since he lived with them, but while unspoken, it was obvious that they still supported him. His place had two bedrooms, a luxury in New York City, especially for a young, unemployed couple. We immediately ingested twenty milligrams of Oxycontin each upon arrival and settled down on the sofa in the bedroom Luca shared with his girlfriend—oddly, the only room in the apartment with a television.

"I'm cold," I said—Luca had kept the AC blasting while he was out—and jumped into his bed, under the covers.

As we watched some shitty movie and our highs kicked in, all three of us ended up on the bed. It was big enough that we could all be comfortable without touching—I was in the middle with Luca on my right and Tom on my left. I thought back to a story Luca had told me once a few years back, about when he and Tom had gone to Spain and had a threesome with a girl they met.

"Her pussy was completely shaved," he had boasted.

"Did she speak English?" I'd asked.

"No."

Upon hearing the story, my first feeling was anger. Not toward Luca or Tom, but toward the girl.

"She let you do that? What was wrong with her?" I asked.

"Nothing, she wanted it!" Luca smiled. "*She's* the one who came on to *us*."

A nice, normal girl seeking a threesome with two guys? No way that was possible. I didn't believe him. Thinking more about it, I decided I hated her. It wasn't something I could explain, but I had a black cloud in my heart for this girl, whose name I didn't know and whose face I'd never seen. The more I thought about her, the darker the cloud grew.

Masking my irrational hatred as pity, I'd told Luca, "That's just sad."

"What are you talking about?" He laughed. "She loved it."

Side by side on the bed, staring blankly at the television, I could see in my peripheral vision that the boys were starting to nod off on either side of me. I thought for a second what it would be like to get fucked by both of them—would it be too awkward? We had been friends for so long; was it too late to spark that kind of emotion? No, I decided. It could be kind of hot. I had tried a threesome with a girl and a guy, and also with two girls. But never two guys—what would it feel like? I had fucked a lot of guys for my young age... I had been called a slut more times than I could possibly count. Would having two dicks at once be crossing the line? What would people say if they found out? What would my girlfriends think of me if I told them?

Fuck. I wanted it.

I don't know what changed in me. Luca had told me the story of the girl in Spain a couple of years before that night, and it wasn't like I had any reason to change my mind since then. I had fucked around with a bunch of guys in those few years, but nothing special. As I sat there, imagining the different positions they could put me in, I realized what I had felt for the Spanish girl was not hatred, not pity—but jealousy. Being someone who had slept with more guys than most of the girls I knew, I considered myself fairly sexually open. Nothing exceptional, but I knew it was enough for others to talk about me behind my back—it was something I struggled with. Sometimes, it made me feel good. I was a "bad girl," a girl who didn't give a fuck what people thought of her, a girl who took what she wanted. Most of the time, though, it made me feel ashamed. Why did I love sex so much? Why did my "number" seem to be growing at a rate four times what other girls' numbers were? It had been a major source of fights between my first love and me—he could never seem to get over the fact I had fucked more people than he had.

Satisfied to be able to put a word to my emotion, I sat in awe of my revelation. It felt good to have an explanation for the black cloud in my gut. I had been envious of the Spanish girl for being able to fuck two guys at the same time. Were things different in her country? Did her girlfriends talk about her when she wasn't around? Did she *have* girlfriends? I realized I had been projecting my own insecurities on her. I hated that part of me, the part that wanted sex, the part I constantly felt I needed to hide. Why should she be able to enjoy it, but not me? WHY NOT ME?

Fuck it.

I turned over onto my stomach, settling the side of my face into the pillow and closing my eyes. Spreading my legs, I started to play footsie with them—my right foot on Tom, my left on Luca.

Slowly, I felt a hand creep up the right side of my back. Then one on the left side.

It was on.

We made out for a long time, me kissing one while the other kissed my neck. Eventually, we were fucking—this was before anal was on the menu, before I even *knew* what double penetration was, so while one fucked me, I either kissed the other or sucked his dick. They didn't seem to mind kissing me after the other one's cock had been in my mouth, and that turned me on. Back and forth, back and forth, they took turns fucking my pussy, fucking my face, and kissing me. It was slow and romantic, the way it always is on opiates. "You look so good getting fucked," one would say to me, looking me in the eyes.

We did this for hours. I should mention here how long a man can last (or can't cum, depending on how you look at it) on Oxys. I, on the other hand, had lost count of how many orgasms I had. After four hours, we decided to take a smoke break. Popping another Oxy as Tom rolled the blunt, Luca suggested we should order Chinese food, and we did. As we smoked blunts and ate our food, it was as if nothing had happened—we were just hanging out exactly as usual, except we were all naked. After we finished eating, now fully in a food coma, we put the empty containers on the floor and fell asleep. Luca and I awoke a couple of hours later and quietly fucked as Tom slept next to us, and eventually joined us again. We fucked until the sun went down, at which point they came in my mouth, at which point I swallowed, at which point we all knew the big event was over. I took a cab home, and each boy texted me individually how hot the experience had been.

That sex changed me forever. I wasn't the same after it, and I knew I could never go back. It was too good—I had enjoyed myself too much. I had spent years being angry at someone I didn't even know for being able to experience something I could only secretly dream about—and finally, that night, instead of envying her, I was able to *be* her. It was so much better to be on this side.

I've told the story of that night to a few people over the years, but not many, because Bella could never find out. Even in retelling it now, I've changed many details so that Luca is unrecognizable. The story usually results in shock and then something along the lines of "You're so crazy." They take it as a confession, when I really mean to be bragging.

I resent that. Upon hearing about our sex that night, people assume I'm the scandalous one in the equation—much like I initially assumed of the Spanish girl. Luca, Tom, and I—we all did the same thing—fucked someone we wanted to fuck. Somehow, when the boys talk about it, they are just *getting laid*. When I talk about it, I've done something *bad*.

"But don't you feel guilty that he had a girlfriend?" some will ask. "You fucked him in her bed."

Honestly, no. Maybe that makes me a cold person, but I really don't think it does. If I had known her, I would have felt ashamed—had she been my friend, or even an acquaintance, I never would have fucked her boyfriend. But I figure that their relationship is his responsibility, not mine.

The truth is that I was just fucking two people I wanted to fuck. To automatically assume I'm the heinous one, not Luca, is upsetting. He was the one betraying someone he loved after all.

I can't help but wonder if it's because I'm a woman. I can't help but know the answer is yes.

Haiku

Slut! Whore! Cum-dumpster!
Worthless shithead! Stupid cunt!
Just don't call me fat

Being in a public space with Spiegler is simultaneously the best and worst. Because he's a porn agent, he's constantly on his phone yelling things like "Your boy/girl scene tomorrow just became anal!" regardless of where we are. Surrounding people turn around to see who we are and are either amused or disgusted. On a good day, this is hilarious. On a bad day, this is mortifying. One time, when he was hospitalized for two weeks after back surgery, I came into his room (that he shared with a stranger) in the morning to find him completely sprawled out, his head at the middle of the bed, legs up in the air crossed, voice-texting someone: "She's done a couple blowbangs, but never a gang-bang—lemme ask how much she'd want for it." He looked up and complained to me that his phone never recognized gangbang as a word unless he separated it into two words, gang and bang. I asked him why he didn't type the text out like a normal human being, but he just shrugged. I think he likes the attention.

We were at lunch in Malibu. Bonnie Rotten had just announced her pregnancy, Carter Cruise had decided she only wanted to do lesbian scenes from now on, and an A-list girl from another agency had just been listed on an escorting site, so we had lots to talk about.

"I wonder what her rate is?" I said aloud as I reluctantly pushed away the bread.

"Why don't you call and find out?"

"I'll ask Dave to do it." Because Dave is a millionaire who loves whores, he is on the VIP list at all of the high-class escorting agencies. He has access to the secret pages of the sites, where the girls who don't want to be identified are listed; this was how we had found out about this particular girl.

I watched Spiegler in envy as he tore apart his bread and ate it piece by piece, slathering butter on it without giving it any thought. *One day,* I thought. *One day, when I'm done with porn, that will be me.* Thoughts like this keep me going.

"You're thinking you're fat, aren't you," Spiegler said with his mouth full. I nodded.

"I can read you like a fuckin' book. Listen, you think you're gonna feel different when you're done with porn, but lemme tell you somethin'—you're never gonna allow yourself to gain weight. You're too fuckin' neurotic. I know you too well."

For once, Spiegler was wrong. Toni and I had made a deal a few years before that when I turned forty, no matter what was going on in our lives, I was going to get fat. I proudly announced this any time the issue of my extreme dieting came up, and I meant it. And here it is now in writing. You'll see.

We moved onto talk about Carter going lesbian only. "Between you going under contract, Jessie, Carter, and Skin going girl/girl-only, and fuckin' Bonnie getting knocked up, the site's gonna be full of girls I can't book," Spiegler sighed.

"We can be called the Spiegler Girl/Girl Girls," I joked.

"Ugh!"

This was my favorite Spiegler expression. "UGH!" A sound

of such disgust, it was comical. It was one that some of the other girls and I had adopted, and now when someone is doing an impression of me, they use it too.

"By the way, guess who's coming back to shooting?"

I thought about it. "Boy or girl?"

"Boy. Well sort of."

"Luke?"

"Yup. I heard he broke up with his girlfriend and now he's back."

"To gay or straight?" Luke was my ex-boyfriend. He did straight porn when we were together and then moved onto gay porn a few months after we broke up. Which I felt was extremely stingy, considering the fact I had begged him to let me watch him at least blow a guy while we were together. He always said no, but at least he let me fuck his ass with a strap-on.

"Apparently straight," Spiegler raised his eyebrows.

"Well doesn't matter to me, cause I am never fucking him again. Not even for money."

"This is why you shouldn't fuckin' date male talent!"

"Ugh!" I exclaimed. "I hate exes. I wish people would just come without exes. Erase them from our lives like in *Eternal Sunshine*." I had said this many times before. I didn't consider myself an overly jealous person, unless it had to do with exes. Not that a person who had never been in a relationship sounded appealing, but...I just couldn't stand the thought of someone I loved having been in love with someone else before me. My intelligent self knew they were exes for a reason; personally, I couldn't stand the thought of going back to anyone in my past.

There was my ex-husband—he was in jail. He owned an underground poker club and was imprisoned for promotion of gambling. Even if he were a free man, there was no way in hell I could be with him. The time I had been with him was practically a black hole in my brain; we spent the entire year and a half on opiates, in a big blur.

My other ex, the one I was with when I had entered the porn business, was an Adderall popper turned alcoholic turned heroin junkie turned methadone addict.

Then there was the other alcoholic, and closeted Luke, and the cute Jewish boy who was never comfortable with my sexual nature or the fact that I was a gentile.

The only one I could've considered being with again was Kevin. But he was dead. Perhaps I only thought of him fondly because of this.

"Do you even know what Toni's ex-wife looks like?" Spiegler asked as his burger and my salad arrived.

I shook my head no, which was half true. I had successfully avoided even knowing her name for a long time, but about a year into our relationship someone let it slip and I Googled her. I saw her Wikipedia page, so I vaguely knew what she looked like, although I wouldn't know it if I passed her on the street. I knew she was Hungarian. I knew she had natural tits. I knew she had gotten into porn with Toni. And if that weren't bad enough—she used to be a Spiegler girl. It was long before I had entered the business; we had never crossed paths. But this knowledge made me want to murder her: my husband AND my best friend? It was too much.

"I think I saw her on a box cover recently," Spiegler continued.

All of a sudden, I could feel every beat of my heart in my chest. For a moment, everything sounded further away than it had a second ago. I sat up in my seat and consciously took a deep breath. "What do you mean? Does that mean she's back shooting again? Or was in a compilation of old scenes?" I already knew the answer.

"I think she's shooting again," Spiegler answered. I leaned back into my seat. Was this a subject I cared to learn about? Definitely. Was it the kind of knowledge that would benefit me in any way? Absolutely not.

I didn't want Spiegler to see how much I cared, so I picked up my fork and started eating my salad, trying to look busy. I tried to think of a way to change the subject, always an impossible task when needed. *Think of something else to talk about... He's going to know you're upset. Say something...anything...*

"Guess who wants to start shooting DP," Spiegler blurted. Thank god.

When Toni came home that night, I had honestly planned on not bringing his ex-wife up. It was the first day of shooting his new movie *Oil and Anal* (title self-explanatory), and I knew he would be tired. So instead we ate dinner, watched a movie, sang karaoke on the PlayStation, and got ready for bed.

"Are you gonna come tuck me in?" I yelled from my bed when I heard him switching off the hallway lights. Every night I asked him this, even though every night I knew he would anyway.

"I had a bad day," I pouted as he sat on my bed. *Oh no. It was happening. I had done so well! It was all going to shit.*

"What's wrong, my skinny princess?" Toni bent down to tickle me.

"Don't!" I screamed. "This is abuse! I'm calling the cops!" I shrieked, laughing. I'm aware this interaction makes it sound like we are in some weird daddy-daughter fantasy relationship, but that's not the case. With Toni on top of me, the words just came out of my mouth: "Did you know your ex-wife is back to shooting?"

Toni stopped tickling me. Looking straight into my eyes, he started smiling the way he does when he's unable to lie or keep a secret. I can't help but find this endearing, and it's gotten him out of trouble a few times.

"Oh, so you know?"

"Yeah, well, Spiegler told me."

"So Spiegler told you he talked to her?"

WHAT?

"Spiegler TALKED TO HER?"

Toni stood up, and I could tell he wanted to turn back time. "Don't tell him I told you! I promised him I wouldn't tell. Wait, so then how do you know she's back in porn?"

"Spiegler told me he saw a box cover of her. Now tell me what the fuck's going on!"

Toni took a breath before he continued. "A few months ago, Spiegler was like *'Guess who's asking me to represent her again. I told her no way, Asa would be mad at me for even talking to her.'* Which you are now! So don't tell him I told you."

I wasn't mad. "Spiegler turned her down? For me?" I couldn't hide my smile. "I can't believe he was able to keep that secret!"

I was no longer upset that Toni's ex-wife was back to shooting. Not for the moment anyway. Spiegler had turned her down, for me, and had managed to keep it a secret to spare my feelings.

It made my day.

HAIKU

I can't help myself
Sometimes when I'm cumming, I
Think of when you're mean

Soapland

Once every month or so, someone I know will text message or email me a GIF that's been circulating on the Internet for a few years now. The looping video is of a woman on her knees, punching a man mercilessly in his testicles, as he ejaculates. With every punch, semen comes squirting out of the man's penis, past the woman's face, and over her right shoulder. The video repeats itself over and over, somehow adding to the grotesqueness of it all.

"Is this you?"

The GIF sent to me is always accompanied by this question. Filmed from behind the woman, it's hard to see her face—you can really only catch glimpses of it from the side, for half a second at a time. The woman definitely looks like me, because it is me.

It was a scene I shot for a company called BallBustingPornstars, for a nice gentleman named Eric who took me out to lunch after I beat his scrotum with my fist.

Before this scene, after this scene, and in the eight years I've been in porn, I feel I can say with confidence that I've officially done a lot. Punch a dude in the balls as he cums? Check. Gangbang? Check.

Double penetration? Check. Anal three-way dressed as a clown? Check, check, check. Yet, out of all the extreme things I've done, the thing I get most recognized for is a very niche-y, relatively softcore website (nurumassage.com), where I cover myself in clear slime and give a full-body massage. Out of the fifty or so scenes I've done for the site, I think I have actual sex in only about four or five. Usually just blowjobs or handjobs; when I got booked for these scenes, I practically counted it as a day off. Sometimes, I'd bang out two or three scenes in a day, just because they were so easy. I'd do my own makeup at home (light and natural, that's how they requested it), show up to the set, throw on a robe (that was the wardrobe), film the scene in an hour, and walk out with a check. The fantasy was that I was the masseuse, and for a "little extra," I would give handjobs, blowjobs, and once in a while, sex. The scene would always start out in the waiting room (in reality, a living room), where I would greet the client. He would tell me he was stressed out from work, needed relief, and I would reply, "My fee is one hundred and fifty dollars. Will that be cash or credit?" (yes, this place took credit). And off we would go to the massage room (bathroom).

Once in the massage room, I would undress my "client," undress myself, and take him to the shower, where I would wash him with a loofah and some cheap hand soap disguised in an expensive-looking dispenser, while avoiding the water splashing the makeup on my face. We'd go from there into the bathtub together for some light handjob stuff, and precisely ten minutes later when beads of sweat would start to trickle into my eyes, I'd leave him in the tub to go get the air mattress from behind the camera. This was the hardest part of the job. Still covered in soap and warm water, I'd have to gracefully walk across the marble floor, grab a slippery blow-up mattress three times my size from behind the camera, bring it back to the center of the room, and elegantly lay it on the floor. The director insisted we always do this in one long shot, rather than using movie magic to just let the mattress appear. I hated this, mostly because my fake tits do something weird when I hold heavy things—or rather, one of them does. My left implant always reveals itself when I do anything that causes any kind of strain on my chest or arms—doing this thing where it turns into, like, three boobs. Because of this, I will never be able to dance topless on a stripper pole. Of course, for the same reason, I cannot get myself up on the pole in the first place.

So once my client is face down on the mattress, I cover myself in the clear slime called "Nuru Gel." Sitting on top of his back like I'm riding in a saddle, I take a moment to let the cold goo slide down my body, before using my hands to slowly rub it all over me. I feel the camera start at my face and slowly pan down, all the way to where my crotch meets his lower back. Once it's focused there, I lower myself onto him completely, rubbing my tits against his shoulders. Here, I whisper something in his ear like "How does this feel, Mr. So-and-So?"

Grabbing his shoulders like handles, I use my entire body to massage his. I flip around, and slide over his back, down his leg, and reach for his foot—then flip around again and come back up. He turns onto his back, and I repeat.

And then I give him a two-minute handjob or blowjob, and it's time to shower and go home.

The first video Toni ever saw of me was from this series. When he came to the U.S. to shoot, it was "the girl in those Nuru Massage videos" he wanted to meet. I've tried to recreate the fantasy for him, only our bathroom/massage room at home is much smaller, and we don't have an air mattress—usually, what ends up happening is us on the cold floor on top of our most raggedy towel. Rather than pouring the gel onto my naked body, without even bothering to remove my shirt, I pour the gel carefully onto his penis (visibly freaking out if it gets anywhere else) and give him the quickest, laziest handjob of his life.

So naturally, when my grandmother was on her deathbed in

Yokohama, my closing statement in convincing Toni to take the trip with me was this: "Just imagine, you can get a real-life Nuru Massage!"

The next day, we were on a flight to Japan. The morning after we arrived, we went to visit my grandmother in the hospital. Tears were shed, touching words were exchanged—I was shocked to see my grandmother in such a state. The women in my family live freakishly long and rarely get sick—whereas the men usually go in their seventies. It's not so hard to see why—the women are so overbearing, I think the men just say, "Fuck it, live the next twenty years by yourself," and just die.

As we left the hospital, my parents suggested we have ramen for lunch.

"Actually, we want to go to Shinjuku," I informed them.

My parents quickly looked at each other. "Why? You just got here, take it slowly," my mother criticized.

"We just want to take advantage of every day that we're here," I explained.

My mother frowned. "But, why are you going to Shinjuku? There's nothing there..."

My father looked down and shook his head, smiling.

They were well aware what we were up to. It was true, Shinjuku wasn't much of a tourist attraction...aside from the prostitutes, hostess clubs, love hotels, and sleazy massage parlors.

"We just want to go, okay?" I snapped. And off we were.

Before leaving the U.S., I had done my research on Japanese massage parlors—or, as they were called there, "soap lands." Many of them didn't service foreigners, but there were numerous lists online of ones that did. I printed out maps so we would be able to navigate by ourselves and wrote down the addresses of a few places in case any were closed.

"I'm so hard just thinking about it," Toni smiled on the crowded train into Tokyo. "I'm excited!"

"I'm so excited *for* you," I smiled back, pressing up against his hard-on.

"I have the best wife," he said into my ear. I leaned my head on his chest as the train rocked back and forth.

Once we arrived in Tokyo, it took us no more than ten minutes to find the first soap land. As Toni smoked his last cigarette by the sign outside labeled DON JUAN, I couldn't contain my giddiness. I shuffled my feet from side to side, doing something like an adult version of the pee-pee dance.

"I think you're more excited than me," Toni said, calmly exhaling the smoke and grinning.

"You have to tell me every single detail. Don't forget anything!" I was jogging in place now. As a woman, I had always been extremely curious about what exactly went on in a real-life, happy-ending massage. Sure, I had been on the giving end of it, in countless pornos—but what was it *really* like? These places rarely serviced women (I've tried), and it was a world I would never know.

"Okay. Let's go up." Toni put out his cigarette on the side of the street and carried it to a trashcan. We would never have taken this kind of care with trash at home in the U.S., but here in Japan, it felt odd to litter—the streets were so clean, the three-second rule could even have applied outdoors. Once, when I had lived there as a child, I threw a tissue on the ground as I walked down the street with my friends. An old lady ran up to me with the tissue, genuinely concerned that I had dropped it by accident. That's how clean the country was: A child throwing her trash on the ground was just unfathomable.

We walked up the dark stairs and entered through some black velvet curtains. Immediately, we were approached by two young men in tuxedos.

"Yes?" They were smiling, but they didn't greet us with the usual "Welcome" or "Irashaimase" standard to every business in the country.

"Sorry," I automatically apologized. I knew going in that, as a woman, I would not be welcomed there. "My husband is a foreigner, and he doesn't speak Japanese—but he would like a massage. Do you service foreigners?" I asked in what was once my primary language. I watched the two young men give each other a quick glance, and I wondered if I had phrased everything correctly.

"Yes, we do," said the one on the left cheerfully, and escorted us through another set of black velvet curtains, to what I supposed was the waiting room. There were mirrors all around, and a television was airing the news. I looked at Toni, and he was already looking at me—we gave each other a look as if to say, "We're in!"

Ashtrays were everywhere. The room was empty.

"Can he smoke?" I asked.

"Yes, please go ahead—I'll be right back."

That was the one thing Toni loved about Japan. Whereas in most countries, people were no longer able to smoke anywhere indoors, here he was able to light up almost anywhere he pleased. It was strange, considering how far advanced the country was in so many ways—it was cleaner than most countries, and the people in general were more civilized than in most countries... even *too* civilized. The people here were polite, and there was hardly such a thing as petty crime. Drugs were highly frowned upon and could earn you years in jail for carrying something as simple as a little pot.

Toni put another cigarette in his mouth, and I lit it for him with a lighter labeled DON JUAN.

"Take the lighter," Toni whispered.

"No, what if there's a camera?" I whispered back.

"Who cares?" Toni gave a deviant smile.

"No," I stood my ground. "People in Japan don't steal."

As if they had heard us, right then, one of the tuxedoed men came back in. "I'm so sorry to inform you of this, but we don't have any girls on staff at the moment to service foreigners." He seemed genuinely sorry.

I had anticipated this. "And...it doesn't matter how much money we offer?" I asked, waiting for his answer to let me know if my offer was sleazy or awesome.

"Sorry, the girls on staff right now don't speak English," he bowed. The Japanese art of apologizing was one thing they certainly had down.

"It's okay," I smiled. "He doesn't care if they can't talk."

The man smiled and sighed. "The soap gets very slippery. There are things she will need to explain to him that are very important."

I knew it was a lost cause, but I pressed on. "It's okay, he's seen this in a million videos—the porno version of this is very popular in America," I explained.

He politely laughed. "I'm sorry, we can't service you. If you'd like to try back tomorrow, or even later tonight, you'd be more than welcome to."

"Thanks," I said. "Can we finish our cigarette?"

"Of course," he smiled and left the room.

"They can't do it?" Toni asked.

"Ugh, no," I frowned. I felt defeated. "Let's go."

We spent the next few hours going up dark stairways, through several velvet curtains, only to be sent back down. Some of the places rejected us the moment we walked in; some wouldn't even let us in at all. With every rejection, I felt worse and worse about my country.

"I'm so sorry," I kept apologizing to Toni on the train ride back to my grandmother's house. "This is so embarrassing. I really wanted you to get that massage."

"It's okay," Toni shrugged. "It's weird, but Japan was a secluded island for a long time," he said, going into a long explanation of the history of my country, while I zoned out into my own thoughts.

How could Japan be seen as one of the most advanced countries and yet be so racist? In so many ways, stepping off a plane into Japan was like stepping off a time machine into the future. The people were more efficient, the advertisements were brighter, and the vending machines sold everything you could possibly need. People stood on the left side of escalators so pedestrians in a rush could pass on the right, and one thing you could never complain about was "Let people exit first before you enter." When you bought something at a store, the cashier *walked around the counter* to hand you your bag. If you were sick with a cold, it was considered the utmost disrespect not to wear a mask over your mouth to protect others from your sickness. How was racism a real thing here in this land of the future?

"I guess you'll just have to settle for my massages on the bathroom floor," I told Toni. I felt I had failed him.

"I like those," he replied. I knew he was simply trying to make me feel better, which made me feel worse.

"I'm so embarrassed for my country. This place sucks," I sulked as the train rattled along.

"Hey, look," he reached into his pocket, and handed me a plain black lighter. "Look on the other side." I flipped it over. There it was in gold writing: DON JUAN.

For the first time in hours, I smiled.

A Letter

It's 5am. This is early for me now. It didn't used to be, not when I was with you... In fact, this is just about when I'd be getting ready for the gym. These days, well most days, I sleep in until I like; I don't even use an alarm clock to wake up.

Suppose I missed you. Would you care? Do you miss me? If this letter reached you, would you just shake your head and mutter "I told you so," tossing it aside in a forgettable corner of your desk? Would you even want to know? Maybe it's because I'm PMSing. Maybe it's that Mercury is in retrograde.

I'm happy now. Really, I am. Everything is going great. There's nothing I can complain about...I feel safe. Loved. I have lots of time to do things for myself. The sex is great. Not crazy, like we used to get, but great—I don't think I need crazy anymore. Great is enough. I have stability. It's such a fucking cliché, but that's something you could never give me... In fact, I have so many things now that you couldn't give me. With you, I lived in constant fear that it would all just end at any second. I don't stay up at night worrying about that now. Many girls would say I'm in the perfect situation. I'm not trying to leave. I don't want to leave. That's not what I'm trying to say.

I think about you more than I care to admit. I see you online, and it's like a punch to the stomach, a pang of jealousy that I keep bottled inside, that I never tell anyone about. On good days, I smile and reason that I can't have everything. On bad days, I block the girls who post about you.

Do you ever reminisce about me? Do you ever think about the six years we had? I can't remember a single bad day. Did we have bad days?

Why did I leave you?

I know what you're thinking: "You made your bed. Now fuck in it."

Meeting you was the best thing that ever happened to me. I can say things like this, now that I'm a woman of thirty. You changed my life. If it weren't for you, I'd be a different person. Because of you, if I dropped dead right now, I'd be okay with that.

But then I think about... What if I want a family? What if I want kids soon? Being with you wouldn't allow for that. You were all-consuming. When I was with you, I didn't have time for anything else. It's a miracle I had time to write my first book. You were all I could think about. You ruled my emotions, how I felt from day to day. When I pleased you, I was happy. When I didn't, I was crushed.

I'm starting to remember the bad days.

Like I said, I'm happy now.

But it would be a lie to say I don't wonder what it would be like if I had never left. A lie to say I don't sometimes just slightly imagine, a teeny tiny bit, what it would be like if I had never signed that Wicked contract. Would we still be together? Certainly on my end, yes. I miss the rush of you, Gonzo Porn. I miss walking into a scene with no idea what was about to happen. I miss fucking as hard as I want, without a director yelling "CUT!" to tell me to tone it down. I miss when fucking was the most important part of the day. I miss getting choked. I miss getting slapped. I miss FUCKING.

I always wanted to be a Wicked Girl. You knew that when we met. I didn't even want you, really... But I fell for you, hard, Gonzo. I thought I was done with you when I got signed. I finally had what I had always wanted.

I'm coming up on two years of shooting only features. It's been really nice. I like my new image...I like when people raise their eyebrows upon my telling them I'm a Wicked contract star. I like being the cream of the crop. You'd think I'd have shaken you off by now! I hope I can shake you off.

It's like they say...it was good while it lasted. You were good for me... No, you were exactly what I needed, at that stage in my life... I suppose I've outgrown you...

I don't know that you need to see this. I don't know that you will. But sometimes, I think about you.

—Asa

Diary

November 18

Toni came inside my pussy last night, and I ran out of douches, so I just left the cum inside of me. The problem is, whenever I do that, my pussy smells like shit the next morning! (I mean that figuratively. Literally, it smells more like a dead animal.) I don't know why this happens with him, I wonder if it means our bodily fluids clash with each other. I hope it doesn't mean we aren't meant to be. And to be clear, him cumming anywhere but inside of my pussy is out of the question. He loves it too much, and it's the only thing I can give him right now that I don't give to anyone else. It's something special.... I've always thought cream pies are romantic, because at the very least, it means you're willing to have his abortion. So for now, I'll just have to douche every time we have sex.

Dee was visiting from Brazil for two weeks, which was super fucking exciting. It had been over two years since we last saw each other, although obviously we speak every single day. She was here just in time for the Hello Kitty convention, which is like… we are both about to be thirty. That was probably our last hurrah, Hello Kitty-wise. Unless we have kids.

We flew out to NYC for a few days, we hadn't been there together in two years. She came with me to Exxxotica in Jersey, then we met up with Dave and Critter in the city for a few days. I kind of wish her and Critter would hook up, he is exactly her type.

I miss her so so so much…no one compares to her. I wish she lived here. Even with her living in Brazil, me in Cali for the last seven years, I still talk to her multiple times every day; I text her more than anyone else in my life. I'm never gonna make another friend like her…I mean she's the closest thing I have to a sister. She's seen me through everything important, ever, and vice versa.

November 19
Seriously procrastinating on packing for my feature-dancing gig in Philly. I fucking hate packing. If sucking a stranger's dick in exchange for having my bags magically packed exactly the way I want them were an actual choice right now—I would take it.

November 22
Back in LA. I told the front-desk guy at the gym that he was hand-some, and now he totally thinks I want him. It's super annoying because now every time I sign in, I'm gonna have to go out of my way not to talk to him or pretend I'm busy looking at my phone. There should be a "no homo" for when we say things that make us sound like we wanna fuck someone, but we really don't.

Is this rape culture?*

*Update: Most definitely not rape culture.

November 25

Yessss! I just got my period! Usually this is not a cause for celebration, but this time it came just in time for Thanksgiving, so I'll be extra hungry and the food will taste extra good.

It's kind of embarrassing how *not* in-tune I am with my menstrual cycle—I'm definitely way too old to be this surprised every time I get my period.

Debating whether this is tweetable or not: *My period is a black guy. Always late and hurts my ovaries.*

November 26

Tweet was a success, seven hundred retweets.

I think I might start Thanksgiving at midnight. The eating part, not the thanking part.

December 4

STORMY LET ME FUCK HER BUTT!

Stormy has never done anal on camera before. But during the scene, she was like "I wonder if this will fit in my ass" and she let me fuck her with this dildo!

Nothing can bring me down right now.

December 5

Just sent Steve Orenstein, owner of Wicked Pictures, this email:

```
From: Asa Akira
To: Steve Orenstein
Subject: BREAKING NEWS

I fucked Stormy's butthole.
```

His response:

Good for you.

December 6

Shot the first episode of *The Sex Factor* today, which is a reality show, much like *American Idol*, but instead of finding the next big singer, we are looking for the next big porn star. I'm the host. I wasn't expecting hot contestants, because if they were hot, helloooo, why are they not in porn already, but to my surprise, they were all pretty good looking. We (me and the four judges) each picked a pair of contestants and "coached" them through their first time fucking on camera. I chose a freaky girl named Mynx who wanted to get DP'd by Charlie and Hero, whom she had met at the meet-and-greet last night. I wanted her to have a good experience, so I secretly gave the boys Cialis an hour before we started to roll. Coaching them through the DP (it was her first) made me kind of miss directing...which is something I didn't think I'd ever say. It's just so much *responsibility*, and there's so much *bullshit* surrounding the actual sex scenes...I don't know. Maybe I'll ask Steve if I can direct something in 2015.

Oh, also one of the contestants showed us how he can suck his own dick. He didn't cum.

December 7

I realized today that I'm like the opposite of a drug addict. While drug addicts are reluctant to admit they are on drugs, I feel the same way about being sober. Not that I'm unhappy about being healthy and clear-minded, but how *uncool* is it to be fucking straight? Corny. Am I right?

In yoga earlier (just to add to the douchiness!), I was remembering the time I went to Bikram Yoga high as fuck on ecstasy. I was having a bad trip, and I had this kid Casey, who I had just met hours earlier, walk me seventy blocks up to the studio so I could "sweat my high out." Once I got there, I realized not only could I not do the yoga poses, I couldn't even stand up in the 106-degree room, so I just laid down for the entire ninety minutes of class.

Fuck, I used to be so cool.

I called Dee to remind her of this. Her reply: "I don't think kids call it ecstasy anymore."

December 10

I'm sick and had to cancel a movie. I feel bad, but it would feel worse to show up to the set sick and expose thirty others to my cold. Plus, I have a lesbian scene in the movie, and a lesbian scene during a cold would just be impossible—first of all, I'd feel bad kissing (which I like to do a lot of, especially with girls.) Second, few things are more torturous than eating pussy with a stuffed nose. It feels like drowning—it's like you have to gasp for air every few seconds. At least with a guy, you're getting fucked, so the time you have to use your mouth is cut by at l east half.

It's weird that if someone cums straight onto your tongue, you won't catch their cold—but if they sneeze five feet away from you, you will.

December 11

Still sick. Watched TV all day. I know I would've been great on *Teen Mom*, because at that age, I thought Ketamina would be a beautiful name for a girl.

Her life: "Ketamina, what a beautiful name, what's its origin?"

"My mother named me after her favorite drug. It's a horse tranquilizer."

December 12

I've been listening to this podcast called *Serial*. It's a true-crime investigation about a murder that happened back in 1999. This seventeen-year-old kid was convicted of murdering his girlfriend, and has been in jail for the past fifteen years. The narrator of this podcast is a journalist, and she interviews the kid (who claims he's innocent), as well as all of the people involved (character witnesses, family members, etc.), and it's clear that there is way too much reasonable doubt for this kid to have been convicted. Plus, in his interviews (they're done over the phone from jail), he sounds so charming... I know, I know, lots of killers are charming (i.e., Ted Bundy), but this kid just has something that really makes me want him to be innocent. And everyone who knows him says they just can't picture him as a murderer...

Which got me thinking. It's really important to be nice to people. You never know when you might be accused of murder and need character witnesses.

It *also* got me thinking—I hate my podcast. That's not to say I don't love doing it— it's still my favorite part of the week when we record *DVDASA*. But I would never, ever listen to us. Everything I hate in podcasts, we do: Our audio is horrible. We talk over each other. We invite guests and then ignore them. We only talk about ourselves. Everything I love in other podcasts, we lack: We don't teach anything. We don't pre-plan anything. We don't have topics.

Are podcasts the new blogs?

December 13

I asked Spiegler today what he would give *Serial* on a scale of one to ten. (I got him hooked on it too.) He said 7.5, which AMAZED me because I'd give it at least a nine—but then I remembered Spiegler only speaks that highly of things that came out a million years ago. *Lawrence of Arabia* is the movie he thinks is the greatest of all time, and when I ask him who's the most beautiful celebrity, he answers Maureen O'Hara. Which is super funny when you're thinking it's a tie between Kim Kardashian and J-Lo.

So I asked him "Has there been ANYTHING worthy of a ten since 1980?" He thought about it for a while, then answered, "Yes. The Internet."

I cannot argue with this. And now I see why nothing, ever, can be a ten again.

December 16

Shot the 2015 Wicked campaign today. Basically, the shots from today will be used for all of next year, as well as at AVN. Wicked always goes big at AVN and plasters huge images of us all over the casino. It's pretty special. Makeup artist gave me a water pill (I think the idea is that it dehydrates you, so you look as skinny/toned as possible) and it turned my pee blue.

December 18

I flew in to Boston today for a dance gig, on a 6:00 a.m. flight. Meaning I woke up at 3:30 a.m. I landed at 3:00 p.m., checked into the hotel at 4:00 p.m., took a nap, and got ready for the gig.

My setup here is kind of crazy—they have my dressing room in an old RV (can't be newer than the '70s) that is parked *outside* of the club. So basically I get to the club, go into the RV, change into a bikini and stripper shoes, leave the RV, *walk outside*, and into the club, onto the stage. I kind of hate it, mostly because it's cold as fuck and those twenty feet between the RV and club feel like needles on my skin.

I made a lot of money.

I'm exhausted.

December 19

Woke up at 1:00 p.m., and watched an eight-part, seven-hour docuseries called *The Staircase* all day until it was time to go to the club. This is what happens to me on dance gigs—I'm literally unable to do anything but lay around in my hotel room all day. Some girls like to go sightseeing, or at least out to lunch or whatever, but I just can't. I'm good for ONE thing a day—that's all I have energy for. So I save it for my job, which starts generally around 10:00 p.m. I usually write and masturbate, in intervals all day long, but today I was especially tired.

December 20

It was my last night in Boston, and it snowed. For the first time ever, I kind of enjoyed it—probably because I knew I'd be flying back to LA in a few hours.

Tonight during the show, I took a beer bottle out of a guy's hand and stuck it in my pussy. I fucked myself with it while all these guys were showering me with dollar bills. It turned me on, it was totally a rush. I had never done that before, I don't know what came over me—I always finger myself, and if the club allows it, I'll fuck myself with a toy—but never some random person's saliva-covered beer bottle. Afterward, I handed the bottle back to the guy, and he chugged the rest of his beer while everyone cheered on. I haven't decided if I'll do it again, 'cause I'm starting to get paranoid that the guy had chlamydia in his throat or something. I'll have to get tested first thing when I get back to LA. If I'm willing to do something so disgusting *sober*, I can't even imagine what I'd be like on these gigs fucked up. I'd probably end up blowing someone on stage. At least.

December 23

Leaving for Cancun tonight! This year for the holidays, Toni and I decided fuck our families, let's go to Mexico alone! Not joking. We were in Barcelona with his family last year, NYC with my parents the year before that... We deserve this, right? Besides, my parents don't give a shit about the holidays, and Spain is just sooooo far away...

Are we shitty kids?

December 27
Ahhhh, I'm getting so tanned, Robert DeNiro might even fuck me.

January 1
Happy New Year!
　　Two more days in Cancun...we spent the New Year just the two of us. We went to bed last night at 9:00 p.m., woke up this morning at 5:00 a.m., fucked, and then went to the beach and watched the sunrise for the first time of the year as semen dripped down my leg. It was perfect.

January 3
Back from Cancun. It was magical. It was nice to be with Toni for ten days straight...we didn't watch TV, we hardly went on the Internet, we didn't talk to anyone but each other. At first I was scared it was gonna be weird...we haven't had alone time like that in a while. But it was really fucking amazing. I'm so lucky he's mine.
　　It's my thirtieth birthday today. I can't believe I've made it to fucking thirty without any Hello Kitty tattoos. Or sex offender registrations. Or cavities! But I've contracted chlamydia like six times, so it's not like I haven't lived.
　　I don't like to celebrate my birthdays really, so we just went to have croissants at my favorite spot in Beverly Hills at 6:00 a.m. We ate them as the sun rose, it was pretty cool.
　　I feel like I should be feeling something, I mean it's my thirtieth birthday. But the day is almost done. And I feel very normal.

January 6
The AVN Convention and Awards Show is coming up at the end of this month. It's the biggest convention of the year for our business...and this year, I've been selected as the keynote speaker. It's

really an amazing thing, I never thought I'd reach this kind of... status? Wrong word. Success? Not really, either... Anyway, it's an honor they hardly ever give to performers (I think the only other one was Sasha Grey), so I'm really feeling the pressure... I haven't even started to write my speech. Starting to get very nervous.

Spring 2015

March 1
Holy shit, it's been a crazy two months. AVN was...interesting. I've hardly even processed what happened. I was the keynote speaker, which almost got taken away. We might be moving. I've been shooting nonstop. I totally haven't even had a chance to write.

Where to begin...

Earlier this month, we found a house we want to buy. We are in escrow. The house is perfect. I don't wanna talk about it too much cause it's not one hundred percent ours yet and I don't wanna jinx it.

Dave is in rehab again. For sex addiction this time. We've been writing back and forth...

Harris Wittels died. He was on our show. And also on heroin. I relistened to the episode... I really clicked with him when we talked about opiates. It was bizarre to hear him talk about getting clean...and I'm realizing most of the people I've known in real life to die have died from some form of opiates.

This past weekend, I had a dance gig in Seattle. I had an allergy attack—okay, rewind actually. Last week, Toni pinched my nipple really hard, and it got infected. It wasn't in a sexual way, or in an abusive way—we were play-fighting. (Just realized this could be a good excuse for covering up for an abusive husband. Not the case, though, I swear.) My nipples were pierced when I was fifteen, and so they're super sensitive. Anyway, so the doctor prescribed me an antibiotic. I'm allergic to most antibiotics, but this one I had taken before and was fine, so I wasn't worried. I was four days into taking them, when I flew out to Seattle for my dance gig.

And as soon as I landed, I started to feel my whole body itching. As soon as I got to my hotel room, I got naked and looked in the mirror. I was COVERED in hives, from my neck to my toes. It was disgusting. I immediately took photos and sent them to everyone I knew. I had Mike (friend/roadie, not the other way around) go get me Benadryl, and knocked out for a few hours before I had go to the club for my gig. Luckily, the Benadryl cleared it up—but I had to take it every six hours in order for the hives to stay away, and I pretty much did the whole weekend gig in a haze. Between lap dances I had to sit down (which is ironic because, hello, lap dance) and I kept thinking I was gonna faint.

I'm home now and finally off of Benadryl...

I'm in a really weird mood though...I can't seem to get out of this funk. I haven't been working out, I haven't really been seeing anyone, I haven't been writing, I haven't even been keeping up with my diary. I haven't been leaving the house much... I've also been eating horribly.

Is this what depression is?

March 3
Holy shit. The house is ours. We got the house. I JUST BOUGHT A FUCKING HOUSE. This is the biggest purchase I've ever made in my entire life. It's probably only the second most important, though—the first was my tits.

I've never lived in a house. In New York City, no one lives in a house—your best-case scenario is a townhouse. Even in Japan, we lived in the kind of house that's connected to other houses. I'm a little scared...

March 4
Bought boxes today to start packing. Our move-in date isn't for another month, but I'm so excited! The first thing I packed is all of my dick-sucking trophies.

March 5
Spiegler got admitted to the hospital last night, we were in the emergency room all day, and tonight he went into emergency surgery at another hospital, they wouldn't allow me there. I've been calling the hospital nonstop, but he's still in there. It's his back. His back has been fucked up for a while, since I've known him really, and they're saying that there's a possibility that...I don't even wanna say it. Okay I can't even do this right now.

March 6
Spiegler is doing great. He got out of surgery late last night/early this morning, and I cried of happiness for the first time in my life, which is something I didn't even know I was capable of. He couldn't feel his legs this morning, which was scary as fuck, but then during the day he regained feeling. He's gonna be in the hospital for a few days; I'm not working this week so I'm glad I can go there every day. When I arrived this morning, he laughed 'cause apparently the nurses told him that "a little kid kept calling to ask about your status." I'm thirty.

March 10
Been at the hospital every day... Spiegler refuses to eat vegetables. He's been eating pizza and hamburgers every single meal! He yelled at me today 'cause I kept begging him to finish the spinach smoothie I made for him. Ugh!

March 11
Spiegler just told me he has never had a mango. In fact he doesn't

even know what one looks like. He's also never seen a kiwi, and he asked me if it's like a "green strawberry." I'm learning so much about him.

March 12
Spiegler got released today, finally. He has a walker thingie, and it's still really hard for him to get around. He's gonna need another surgery in a few months, but for now he's good, and he should be able to walk without the walker thingie pretty soon.

March 18
I'm in Florida for a signing. I stand by my theory that this is the trashiest state in the country. There are a lot of people named Randy here.

March 20
Back in LA. Feeling sick.

March 26
Heading to NYC tonight for a dance gig, then gonna stay with my parents for a few days. I wish New York were less conservative, cause then I could fuck myself on stage to the theme song of "The Jinx."

March 28
Danced last night at Sapphire. I had lunch with Jules yesterday before my show, and when I told him I was here for a feature-dance gig, he asked me: "Is that like a recital?"
    I died.

April 6
Back in LA. I couldn't find my razor this morning, so I used Toni's to shave my pussy. OH MY GOD why didn't anyone tell me how

much better men's razors are? It has me questioning everything now...WHAT *ELSE* HAVE I BEEN DOING WRONG ALL MY LIFE?

April 8
I've been in Canada for two days, shooting a commercial for Wicked with Chanel Preston. I haven't been here since I was a grouchy teenager, and I have to say I fucking love it here. Everyone is so *polite*. Like, I noticed whenever I say thank you here, they don't reply with "You're welcome." Oh no. They say "You're *so* welcome!" and when someone bumps into you, they actually say "Sorry!"

April 9
Um, nevermind everything I said about Canada yesterday. Today we were at lunch and Brad Armstrong (the director) got bombarded by fans; Chanel and I have not been recognized a single time since we've been here.
    I'm ready to leave now.
    I'm just kidding. Sort of. Not really.

April 12
The last awards show of the season, XRCO, was last night. They've been really good to me in the past; they're the only show that's crowned me twice as performer of the year. This year I won mainstream media favorite. Bleh.

April 16
Something I never thought I would say: "I'm in Oklahoma!"
    But it's true. I am. Dancing here for three nights.

April 20
Aside from it being 4/20 (who cares) and Hitler's birthday (semi-

interesting), today is the best fucking day ever. Toni's shooting an oil movie next month, so he bought a see-through kiddie pool—actually, he bought four. This type of thing has been happening a lot since he got Amazon Prime. I think the free shipping and "buy with one click" is just too tempting for him to resist—last week a T-shirt he ordered came, and it ended up being a child's extra-large, not adult. So that was a free shirt for me. A shirt I didn't want, but somehow I've been wearing for a week straight now. And this time, it's a free kiddie pool for me! Another thing I didn't want, but we blew it up for fun today before he went to work. It's huge and amazing. (That's what she said.) I'm not sure we even need to put in a real pool! $49.99 instead of $49,000.99 is sounding pretty fucking good right now.

Let me go over how my day was: I woke up at 6:00 a.m. Made coffee, wrote for six hours straight. That's "not wrote" for one hour and Googled random shit for five hours, but actually wrote for six hours straight. That's more than enough for me to be high on for the rest of the day, but then I went out to the backyard, turned on *This American Life*, and went in the kiddie pool. I stayed there for two hours, in and out of a nap, listening to podcasts...and I got a nice tan.

I came back into the house, made a delicious smoothie, wrote for another hour, and then Toni came home and we fucked. Now we just ordered Italian food. I LOVE MY LIFE, CAN EVERY DAY BE LIKE THIS?

April 21
Major writer's block. I feel so fucking depressed. Bye.

April 24
I'm over a month due for Botox, I called to make an appointment today, and MY BOTOX LADY IS OUT OF TOWN UNTIL NEXT WEEK. We start production on Magic Mike XXXL

TOMORROW… Fuck. I sat in front of the mirror for over an hour just now, obsessively moving my forehead up and down. I hate when it can move.

April 25
I fucked Bridgette B today… Well, we did a four-way, so I didn't get to fuck her as much as I would've liked. She's probably the hottest girl in porn for me… She's Spanish, super tanned, with bleached blonde hair, and HUMONGOUS tits. She got to the set today and the production manager had forgotten to send her a script… I gave her mine, and before she even looked at it, was like "Let me guess. I'm playing a hooker."

I was like, "Nope! It's your lucky day! We're playing porn stars. So, we pay taxes."

May 1
Putting my wardrobe together for my shoot tomorrow. There's a funeral scene in this movie, in a porno movie. What is the appropriate attire for a funeral scene in a porno? I need something that says "I'm paying my respects." But also, "I'm DTF."

May 5
For the last three days, I've been shooting *Deception*. Stormy and I have an interesting relationship in that she is mean to me, and I love it. There's a certain kind of meanness I work really well under, and I can't quite put my finger on it—but she has it. Today, she even made me ride a stick-horse naked around the room on camera for an audition for her next movie. (A movie I don't even want to be in, BTW: it's a Western. I hate Westerns. I hate horses. I hate nature. I hate wearing big costumes. Did I mention I hate Westerns? Oh also, I'm Asian. So basically I'd be a railroad worker or an Indian.) She was torturing me particularly hard on this set, and the only light at the end of

the tunnel for me was the spinach dip that my male costar Jack had brought to the set for me, which I was looking forward to eating all day.

But tonight, at 1:00 a.m., after I had wrapped, in a rare moment of kindness Stormy let me jump in on a scene with her and Kleio Valentine. It went something like:

> Me: "Yayyyy I'm done! I'm gonna go home now and eat this entire thing of spinach dip! Oh Kleio, when did you get here? Are you shooting tonight?"
>
> Kleio: "Yeah I'm shooting a lesbian scene with Stormy!"
> Me: "Is it for this movie?"
>
> Stormy: "No, it's for the showcase I'm doing, there's no dialogue so I'm collecting scenes slowly. I wanted to put you in it but I didn't wanna make you shoot two scenes in the same day. Unless... Do you wanna join us?"
>
> Me: *Drops all my bags* "What should I wear?"

The scene was awesome. I mean who would pass on the opportunity to fuck Stormy and Kleio? AT THE SAME TIME? Driving home, I texted Stormy. `Joke's on you, none of your meanness from the past three days matters anymore because I got to fuck you!`

I put my phone away in my bag and continued driving, feeling all smug, like I had just won a weeklong battle. When I got home, there was a text from Stormy. I imagined she was admitting her defeat. I opened the message.

`Joke's on who?`

Under the text was a photo of her with her tongue sticking out. HOLDING MY SPINACH DIP.

NOOOOOOO! I texted back. FUCK!

`I took your ass and your dip, bitch.`

`You vagina trapped me. It was all a distraction`

so you could get my dip. You're even more evil
than I thought!
Haha. True.
I love Stormy.

May 6
Flew to Hawaii this morning, I'm dancing tonight and tomorrow
here in Honolulu. I love this place... I always plan on extending
my stay here and taking a vacation with Toni after my dance gig,
but it never fucking works out. Maybe it's for the best 'cause Dave
has a theory that all couples break up in Hawaii.

May 7
Out on the balcony of my hotel room, overlooking the gorgeous-
ness that is Hawaii. I swear, it's impossible to take an ugly photo
here. I could just close my eyes, spin around three times, point
my camera in a random direction, and the photo would come out
beautiful.

I was excited to write all morning in this atmosphere, but so
far all I've done is Google myself for two hours.

May 9
People on Twitter keep wishing me a Happy Mothers Day. Does
this mean they see me as a MILF? Don't they know none of my
children made it past the first trimester?

May 11
Just got back from the gym. I saw an old Asian lady there in her
street clothes, and she was bossing around her muscle-head son,
making him set up all her equipment. I was like awwww, maybe
that'll be me one day. Kind of made me wanna have a kid.

May 15

We've been shooting *The Sex Factor* for the past week. The whole production has been a little bit of a shit show, but I suppose that's to be expected when the premise is *American Idol*, but with porn stars.

It's been a lot a lot a lot of fun... Keiran is one of the judges, and that's always a good time; he's one of my favorite people in porn. Probably because he is basically the same person as me. Lexi Belle is a judge too, and she's such a fucking mystery to me... like, right when I think I have an understanding of who she is, she says something that just throws my theory right out the window. People think she is all sweet and innocent because of her blonde hair and adorable face, but she is secretly fucking evil! She tells some of the most cold-hearted jokes. And then right when I think she has no soul, she cries when a contestant gets eliminated. That actually happened today. She told me not to tell anyone, but I'm fucking telling everyone.

May 16

A contestant said today that the freakiest thing she's ever done was have a boy pee on her in the shower. I feel like...if you're in the shower with a boy, and he *doesn't* pee on you, he's not that into you.

May 19

This was the last day of *The Sex Factor*. We officially have two winners, a boy and a girl. I think the right people won.

May 20

Thought of a really good "Would you rather." WOULD YOU RATHER...be middle class and deaf, or rich as fuck and incurably blind? Because deaf versus blind is way too easy, of course everyone picks deaf. Dee and I decided it wouldn't be so bad if

147

we got blind together, but we were really rich. We could just lay in bed all day, doing heroin, talking, listening to podcasts. Since we'd be rich, we could just have a twenty-four-seven staff on hand to do everything for us. And we could eat whatever we wanted, because hello, we are blind and together, who cares if we get fat.

May 22
Thought of a really good relationship test: Leave your used fake lashes around the house. If your boyfriend freaks out, it means he hasn't fucked enough sluts to be true relationship material yet.

May 23
Starting a new showcase movie tomorrow—meaning, an all-sex movie with all five scenes starring me. I'm really excited, I'm fucking a lot of my favorite men: Toni in an anal scene, Mick Blue and Karlo Karrera in a DP, and Rob Piper, Tyler Knight, Moe the Monster, and Jon Jon in a blowbang that I'm secretly hoping will turn into a gangbang, if Wicked allows it (I doubt it though, they haven't let me do a gangbang in the two years I've been with them). The only problem with doing a blowbang with four black dudes is that my hard-earned tan literally pales in comparison. Oh well.

Summer 2015

June 23
Just got back from two weeks in Spain with Toni and my parents. For the most part, it was great. It was our parents' first time meeting, and they LOVED each other—I think his parents probably like my parents more than they like me. I never really thought about it, but our parents' dynamics are really similar: still together, bossy overbearing mom, passive, happy-go-lucky dad. We spent most days all together as a family, it was really nice.

Toni's house is being rented, so when booking the trip, Toni and I thought it would be fun to rent an apartment for us and my parents to stay in together, rather than booking separate hotel rooms. I'm not sure why we thought this—right before the trip, we were like "Why the fuck did we do that?" Neither of us could remember.

We had separate bedrooms, obviously, but being in the same apartment afforded us no time away from my parents, and even worse, it afforded me personally NO TIME ALONE. This was a disaster. At home, Toni and I have separate bedrooms, bathrooms, and offices. What made me think I could survive two weeks in a tiny apartment with three other people?

At the end of the first week, I had a meltdown. We had just gone to the Gaudi Museum, my mom was being really overbearing, I had had ZERO time to myself, and I was really starting to be in a bad mood. I can recognize when I'm about to be a nightmare, and I'm pretty good about just going to find my own space and leaving everyone alone until I feel better. We were driving to lunch, when I found out we were going to be eating at Toni's friend's restaurant. I asked, "Can we go somewhere else? I'm feeling really grouchy, and I'm gonna be a total bitch if we have to talk to people." I know this sounds horrible and cold and totally cunty, but really, I was trying to spare Toni the embarrassment of having a shitty wife.

Toni and I started going back and forth about it, but not bad—like on a scale of one to ten of arguing, one being a playful bickering about TV characters, ten being us throwing things at each other, this was like a two or three max. My mom butted in, and I lost it. "Please stay the out of this, I'm arguing with Toni right now!" I turned into the worst thirteen-year old version of myself. I started crying, screaming at everyone, "I just need to be ALONE! You're all driving me fucking insane!"

We parked outside the restaurant, and I refused to get out of the car. Everyone went in without me, and I sat there by myself, crying, smoking, and emailing with Spiegler. I knew I was way too old to be acting like that, which just made me cry even harder. Toni came out and calmed me down, saying he understood, I didn't need to go in if I didn't want to, I could sit there and cry if I wanted, but I couldn't yell at everyone like that. I ended up going inside and apologizing to everyone, which is just about the hardest thing in the world for me to do. The next day Toni went to hang out with his friends, my parents went sightseeing by themselves, and I walked around Barcelona by myself all day. It was the best. There's something about walking around a foreign country by yourself...it's the most anonymous, magical feeling. I feel the most empowered when I do this.

The rest of the trip went smoothly with no tantrums.

June 25
I think it's dumb that we say "bless you" every time someone fucking sneezes. I mean, it's one thing if you believe in god and you really believe that thing that when you sneeze, your soul is trying to escape—but I don't. Why am I saying bless you?

I'm from a family of sneezers. My mom and I both get hay fever pretty badly. Sneezing was a big part of my formative years, and it continues to be a big part of my life now. It's gonna be a hard habit to break, but I'm gonna do it.

June 27
Writing a book is fucking hard. I'm so thankful, and as much as I hate to use this word—*blessed*—to have the opportunity to even write such a phrase. But fuck...I feel like I'm on drugs again. I wake up every morning and (attempt to) write. Yesterday was a good writing day. I wrote one fiction chapter and 1,800 words of an essay. About four thousand words total. I felt invincible the rest of the day...I even went to get that oil change I've been putting off for six months/five thousand miles.

But today...I sat in front of the computer from 6:00 a.m. 'til now (8:44 a.m.) and wrote fucking nothing. I changed a couple of words in the essay I started yesterday, but that's it. Nothing significant. I feel like a piece of shit. I'm so depressed. I feel like a failure. None of this is an exaggeration...I forgot how much writing rules my emotions.

I texted my mom just now: "I miss you. I'm very homesick today."

I'm trying to think of something that will make me happy... and I can't. The only thing that would please me right now is to write something amazing. But it's just not happening. I Googled "INSPIRE ME" and all I got were a bunch of memes.

I want to take a nap.

No, I don't.

In moments like this I think of Dee a lot. I really miss her. I miss having a true friend around.

I also think of back when I didn't have money. Dee and I would always say, "It wouldn't be so bad if we had money." Going through a breakup, being depressed, getting off drugs... Now I see that while it would have made a difference, it wouldn't have saved me from feeling like this.

I'm telling myself things like "I'll buy you anything you want, we can go anywhere you like, how about a massage? Acupuncture? Spa day?" Even "you can cheat on your diet today."

But I don't want any of it. I just want to write. But wanting to write is not enough. Motivation is not enough.

They say writing is therapeutic. *I've* said writing is therapeutic. What they don't tell you is that being unable to write is the exact fucking opposite. What's the word for the opposite of therapeutic? I'm sad.

I need something to happen to me. Even if it's horrible. I need content. I immediately regret saying that. Cancel cancel cancel.

This is torture.

June 28

It's almost embarrassing how unaware I am of when I'm getting my period. I'm too old to be this surprised every month! The signs are always there: I get depressed, I get grouchy, I even ordered pasta last night in a fit of uncontrollable hunger (okay, maybe that just happens all the time) and when I woke up this morning—boom, blood on my underwear. (I wonder if once I'm off the birth control, the PMS is gonna get like HORRIBLE? A little scared.)

I feel better today. I mean it's only 7:00 a.m. so we'll see.

I watched a documentary last night, *Happy Valley*, about a *Friday Night Lights*-type town (only it was college football instead of high school, so even more extreme) where the assistant football coach raped (at least) ten young kids, and the head coach knew about it and didn't report it to the police. The head coach was treated like a god in this town, so it was super controversial. We never found out why he didn't alert the authorities, because he died three months after the story came out, before he could go to court or anything. Maybe he didn't report it because he thought it would ruin the town spirit? Maybe he was just an asshole? Maybe he was in on it somehow? Maybe the assistant coach was his best friend? It would suck to be a pedophile. I wondered if Dee were a pedo, would I report her? I texted her:

I just watched "Happy Valley". If I were a pedo, would u report me to the police? I don't think I'd report u. I'd like to think I'm the kind of person who would, but I don't think I would. You are way more correct than me though, ethically.

Dee's in Rome right now so her service is choppy and also there's the timezone difference. She hasn't replied yet.*

I know it's horrible. I think the head coach in *Happy Valley* is a monster for not reporting the assistant coach. If Toni were fucking children, I would report him. If *anyone* were, I'd report them. But Dee...I don't know. I really don't know.

Being a pedo would suck so fucking bad. Like having a fetish that's morally/ethically wrong...ugh. I'm so lucky. If I were a pedo I think I'd just kill myself. Initially, I thought, "Oh easy, I'd just do massive amounts of heroin and keep myself sedated," but opiates make me horny, so I think that would be too dangerous.

By the way, I've totally been saying "bless you" every time someone sneezes around me. It's like a Pavlovian reaction. I always remember immediately after, but by then it's too late, there are no takebacks on saying bless you. This is going to be even harder than I thought.

*Update: Dee wrote back. Hahaha I don't know. I would try not to.

I think she's just being nice. Dee is the most ethically correct person I know. She is so stubbornly progressive, she will break up with a guy at even a hint of homophobia. Which I applaud her for! I wish I could be that strong.

June 29

Had a major scare last night. Around 11:00 p.m., my dog Homie started shivering, and when I went to hug him, his whole body was completely tense. I cried and called Toni who was at work, he couldn't leave—so I Googled, which of course always says the C word. I took him to the emergency vet, which luckily is super close—and three hours, two x-rays, one blood test, and six hundred dollars later, they told me that Homie is just old and fat. His body was tense and he was shaking because he was consti-pated. They gave me laxatives and antibiotics (not sure why the antibiotics) and told me to switch him to senior dog food.

Not sure if I was projecting, but I was offended when the doctor called him fat.

June 30

Dana (DeArmond) came over yesterday; she hadn't seen the new house yet. She is my favorite person in porn.

Dana's fucking a celebrity, which I think is more exciting for me than it is for her—I bombarded her with a million questions. What does his penis look like? (Big.) What is the sex like? (Good, not weird.) What do you guys talk about? (Normal stuff.) I always assume celebrities are into really weird sex, maybe because they get so much of it? I suppose it is an unfair generalization, especially since it's completely not based on any kind of facts. I've never fucked a celebrity, and I feel like maybe I never will. I've had a lot of famous people hit on me on Twitter and Instagram, but like...I don't know, I've just never been interested in meeting any of them in person. There was one I would've fucked, but I was already married by the time he hit on me. And really, I'm not sure if I really even wanted to fuck him—I really just want to eat pizza while he tells me jokes. (He's a comedian.) If I could fuck any celebrity I'd probably just wanna get DP'd by the ATL twins, and that's more just because they are twins that DP together, not because they are (pseudo)famous.

Dana has been single for about a year now, and I completely live vicariously through her. She's on Tinder, which seems both super fun and super dangerous at the same time. Like I feel like if I were a rapist, Tinder would be awesome. She sends me dick pics and screenshots of funny texts. For completely selfish reasons, I hope she's single forever. But when she finds someone she wants to be with, I hope he is cool so Toni and I can be couple friends with them.

July 8

Had the bestest, most funniest idea ever for when awards season is here. It's like fantasy football but instead of players, you draft porn stars, and every time someone on your fantasy porn star team wins an award, you get a point. Dana is on board. Spiegler says he will play as long as there are no paper trails leading back to him. He also says I have too much time on my hands. Now all I have to do is learn how fantasy football works.

July 12

Started shooting Brad's movie yesterday. I did a dialogue scene in the pool, then had an anal three-way with jessica and a male talent.

While we were fucking, the male talent kept whispering in my ear about fucking his ass with a strap-on. It was really hot... It made me kind of miss doing that. My last boyfriend Luke loved it, but Toni won't even let me put a finger in his asshole. I keep saying I will turn him one of these days.

Today is my only shoot day with no sex, just dialogue, but it should be fun because it's a big party scene. Spiegler is gonna bring the new girl by to be an extra so she can meet Brad.

Oh, also my asshole is torn.

July 18

We wrapped the movie last night around 2:00 a.m. My last scene was with jessica drake. I swear every time we work together in a one-on-one lesbian scene, we just end up fucking like crazy and forgetting about the cameras. It's insane.

I also worked with Tommy Pistol for the first time the day before. He is fucking amazing. He likes getting his foreskin bitten really hard, and it was so hot. That guy is really good at fucking. I will definitely be requesting him again.

It's raining here today. My Twitter feed is full of people like "I love this weather! I love when it rains!" and I'm like what the fuck... it rains all the time in NYC and I fucking hate it, it's so inconvenient. I think people in LA love it so much because one, it only rains like five times a year here, and two, no one has a real job, so everyone can just stay in their houses in pajamas and order pizza.

I am in my pajamas and pizza is on the way.

July 26

Just got home from a dance gig in San Diego. The club said I broke records all three nights, but I never know whether or not to believe them when they say that. Do they just tell every girl that? Not sure.

The gig went great. I took Stevie as my roadie for the first time, and I have to say...it was really nice being on the road with a girl. I had never done it, and to be honest, I was skeptical...I don't even like when my Uber driver is a girl. Not because I hate girls, but because I feel bad asking them to carry my suitcases and stuff. But it was awesome. She was really fun, and I feel like I definitely sold some extra lap dances thanks to her. I usually don't like to do anything during the day but write in my hotel room, but with Stevie I actually called her to hang out a couple of times.

July 29

Okay, so on a whim, I did something crazy yesterday. There's a medical spa right underneath boot camp, and my friend Annie works there, so sometimes I go in just to say hi. She's usually able to sell me on something. I had been wanting to try this thing called ultherapy, which is like a laser thingie for anti-aging treatments. They pulse these radio frequencies into your face to produce more collagen. So I did it.

That's not the crazy part.

I also decided to get my lips done!

I had to BEG Toni to let me do it. Not that I needed his permission, but I know how he feels about when I do these kinds of things (he fucking hates it) and I wanted to be considerate, since he is the one who has to look at my face all the time.

He FINALLY agreed. We came to a compromise that I would

try just a LITTLE bit, and if he didn't like it, I would never do it again. (Like Botox, the results fade in three to nine months. I just told him three, though.)

August 17
Holy shit, what a week it's been. I went back to LA from Dallas, was home for one day, and then came to San Francisco, where I'm dancing this weekend. I got in touch with my friend Perry who I haven't seen in over ten years...so crazy. We went to middle school and some of high school together, and he was actually the first person I smoked weed with. We are both "sober" now (I put that word in quotes not because we aren't completely sober, but because the word just sucks...it sounds pretentious and gross), and he is a photographer. He has a daughter that he loves a lot, and honestly he seems like a really great dad. We talked about who's gay, who's dead, who's in jail...neither of us went to the ten-year reunion. He said "it's cool to see how we've changed in some ways and remained the same in others," and I found that crazy poetic. We messed around a lot in school, but never fucked. I don't think he was at all shocked to find out I'm in porn now.

The club has been crazy packed. I always do really well at this club in San Francisco, and it seems like it gets even more crowded every year. It's always standing room only, and the energy here is great. Plus, it's a full nude club that lets me do whatever I want onstage, so I usually bring a dildo up with me. If the crowd is particularly awesome, I usually I get so turned on and excited that I end up handing the dildo over to someone in the crowd and asking them to fuck me while surrounding people shower me with dollar bills. It's fucking exhilarating in a way that nothing else is. I did that last night to someone, and later during the meet-and-greet, I found out that he was there with his stepdad, who was sitting right next to him as he fucked me. I went through something like the five stages of grief, but totally different. First

I was horrified. Then I was apologetic. But I realized he really wasn't that weirded out by it, so I started laughing like crazy, and genuinely found it funny. After the night ended and I was back at the hotel, I realized that was the closest I'd ever come to actual incest. And I felt awesome.

Fall 2015

September 6

Wrapped my showcase *Asa Goes to Hell* last night. Some highlights:

Eric John caught on fire while he was fucking my ass. The premise was that I'm in hell, so we had fires going all around us—and he knocked one of them over. Everyone is okay.

I worked with Aiden Ashley for the first time. Holy fuck she was amazing. After our scene, she tweeted that I have the most decadent asshole she's ever eaten. Still riding on this high.

In total, I took six loads on my face, and NO cum got in my eye. This is highly suspicious, and I'm starting to worry that something terrible is about to happen to me.

September 7

Went to see *ET* last night with Dana and Spiegler. It was playing at the Hollywood Bowl, and the Philharmonic played the score live. It was so moving, I cried from the opening scene.

September 13

I'm going to cry. So, Spiegler had his spine surgery scheduled for October 13th. I had scheduled everything accordingly—going to a dance gig October 9-10, then coming home on the eleventh and taking the rest of the month off to take care of Spiegler.

Well they MOVED HIS SURGERY UP to October 9th. Meaning, I won't be there when he wakes up. It's fucking killing me. I tried to move the gig but they couldn't. And I've already signed the contract, so if I don't go I'll have to pay them like a million dollars. He says it's fine, that it's pointless for me to be here during the surgery anyway. And I suppose he's right. It's fucking killing me.

September 15
Okay so I've been afraid to say anything, I didn't wanna get my hopes up for nothing, or worse, jinx it. Toni has officially quit smoking for fifteen days now. I'm so fucking elated about this. I haven't smoked a cigarette since June 1st, and I feel great—if Toni quits smoking, it'll pretty much guarantee I won't start up again. Living with a smoker, when you're an ex-smoker, is torture.

He smells better, he's more energetic, I'm so so happy. I bought him a new camera to celebrate fifteen days. I'm also secretly hoping it will guilt him into continuing this great streak.

September 18
I'm on a dance gig in Richmond, Virginia. One of my closest friends from high school (we are merely Facebook friends now) lives here, and her family were founders of the city. I wonder if I'll see her name anywhere? I'll keep my eye out.

September 21
Back from dancing. Met new Spiegler girl. We paid for her lunch; all she said was an automatic "thank you." It wasn't worth saying anything over (we were eating at CPK not Fleming's) but later in the Apple Store, Dana and I agreed we would never forget this.

September 22
Toni and I are in a pedometer war. We've both been wearing these clip-on devices (very, very cool and hip) that measure our steps—both of us have set our goals to ten thousand, which is

pretty easily achievable if I go to boot camp that day. Toni has won every single day EXCEPT YESTERDAY. I beat him by two thousand steps, which I added in by deciding to mop the floors at 10:00 p.m.! It's not easy being in any kind of physical war with Toni, because he is naturally just a more physical person than me—he's the kind of person who even when he's just standing is not standing *still*. I am the exact opposite—my personal motto is "Why stand, when you can sit?"

September 23
Just booked tickets to NYC, leaving in a week. I haven't been there in over a year...so crazy, I didn't even realize because my parents have been coming to LA, and we also took that big trip to Spain together a few months ago. I'm shooting there with this photographer Stacy, whom I've never met in real life, but she's my new friend. Like all great and safe relationships, this one started on Instagram—she kept tagging me in these photos she took of my RealDoll. She's doing an exhibit in November, a project solely of dolls. I was intrigued so I DM-ed her, asking her if she'd be interested in shooting me with my doll. I'm pretty excited! Hope I'm not getting catfished, and it ends up she's actually a creepy rapist! Either way, it'll be nice to go home before Spiegler has his surgery.

September 26
So, a new offer came on the table. I hardly even want to talk about it yet, because who fucking knows what will happen, but at this point I'm not taking it too seriously.

Next month, in October, my annual Wicked contract is technically up. I signed on two years ago for a one-year deal. We renewed last year for another year, and I think we are both assuming we will renew again this year. But the day before yesterday, another company (I seriously don't even want to say which at this point) started an interesting conversation. It's one of the other biggest companies in porn right now. There are lots of pros and cons... for one, I always wanted to be a Wicked girl. This was my dream from the beginning. But Wicked has a very concentrated audience...for lack of a better word, it's "classy" porn. It's made with a target audience of couples in mind, and they're known to only shoot the most beautiful, most well-spoken girls in the business. It truly is an honor to be one of their three contract girls.

However, it doesn't do much to keep my name out there. The other company showed me some Internet stats: before I signed with Wicked, I was the number-two most searched porn star worldwide. (Number one, of course, was Lisa Ann.) My ranking has slowly declined, and now, two years after signing, I am number seven. By this time next year, who fucking knows where I'll rank. I'm not gonna lie, this fucking crushes my soul. I knew it would happen. I just didn't think I'd care.

The new company is pretty much guaranteed to get me back in the top three. They're offering more money, but it's also more work. It would mean less time for writing, and instead of slowing down (which was one of the major perks to signing in the first place), I'd be busy as fuck again.

I gave them my counteroffer (is that the word?) and list of demands, and if they can meet it, I'll seriously consider it. Otherwise, I'm perfectly happy at Wicked, so I won't budge.

September 28

I've been on hold with the IRS for almost four hours now. SINCE 6:00 A.M. UGH. Is there anything worse? Yes, yes there is: watching my mom Google. But this is a close second.

Because in porn we are freelance/1099 employees, every year, I pay my estimated taxes, then file for an extension, and then call the IRS for my income transcripts in both my name and corporation, so that I can get the exact number I owe. Personal and corporation are two separate numbers, so it's double the phone time. We get most of our 1099s in the mail, but a good one-third of them don't make it—and MY WORST NIGHTMARE is not paying enough taxes, or worse, getting audited. I hate hate hate doing this. But it beats the possible alternative.

Today is Spiegler's birthday. He doesn't like people to know, though. I'm gonna call him when (IF?) I finally get off the phone with the IRS.

September 29

Oh my god, two big things:

Yesterday (when I finally got off the phone with the IRS), I went to boot camp and this guy from my favorite soap opera of all time was there. That's not the big news, he's always there. So we were both there early, warming up, when in through the door walks ANOTHER GUY FROM THE SHOW. So obviously I was watching them very closely, thinking like *ooh, what is THIS conversation going to be like*, and guess what...THEY DIDN'T EVEN SAY HI TO EACH OTHER. There was one point during class when they walked RIGHT by each other, I mean like inches within each other, and they didn't even lock eyes. SCAN-DALOUS! They must totally fucking hate each other. This is the most exciting thing that's happened to me in a very long time.

The second thing is that someone tweeted me a link today. I opened it, and it was a video from some new station in North Carolina where my ex-boyfriend Luke was proposing to his girl-friend at the elementary school where she teaches. It was so weird to see him in the interview, he was all excited to propose, he was wondering if he should do it in a church... I know, I know, I cannot believe he goes to church. He told me he didn't believe in god, what a fucking liar. I don't know why I'm surprised though, everything else he told me was a lie...he even faked his mom's death once to get me to come home early from a party. AND HE KEPT THAT LIE UP FOR A YEAR AND A HALF. He's not in porn anymore; in fact, after a short stint in gay porn, he moved to NC and started a Crossfit gym or something. And now he's dating an elementary school teacher, good for him. I wonder if she fucks his ass better than I did.

September 30
Talked to the other company again, got into a little bit more detail about what exactly their contract would entail. Told Steve (owner of Wicked) about it... Although I'm still treating it like a joke, I felt like shit talking to them without Steve knowing about it.

I'm flying to NYC tonight to meet my new friend Stacy who's gonna shoot me with my RealDoll. Still half scared she is a murderer. I'll know for sure in twenty-four hours!

October 1
The good news is I'm alive, Stacy was not a murderer, she's awesome, we got some really cool photos, and I hope they are good enough for her show in November!

The bad news is, I FORGOT MY FUCKING PEDOMETER IN LA. What's the point of even walking? Ugh. At least it's raining here, and I'm at my parents' house—I'm probably not gonna be doing much walking anyway.

After the shoot today, I went to dinner with Julian, Sara, Peter, Peter's new boyfriend Philip, and Stephanie. I miss living here. : (

October 3
Somehow my mom convinced me to apply for a credit card. And I did. I've never had a credit card before...I know, it's crazy. I'm super terrified.

October 4
Holy fucking shit, the most bizarre thing happened.

So I was sitting at the gate in the airport to come back to LA, when this cute guy walked past me. We locked eyes so I smiled, and he smiled back. He looked really familiar but I couldn't decide if one, I knew him, two, he was famous, or three, he just had that kind of face. Right after I smiled, this other totally random lady was like "Hi Asa!" and I said hi back. The cute guy heard her say my name, and so he walked up to me and said, "I know you."

So I said, "I think I know you too! What's your name?"

"Mark. I played drums in the subway."

It's so crazy. So I met him in 2004 (we figured this out after Googling what year *Kill Bill 2* came out, it was a movie we went to see on a date) when I was nineteen. He played the drums (with his hands, that's his thing) at Union Square on the L train platform, and I always saw him when I was going home. One day he gave me his CD and told me his email was on the back. I'm not sure if I emailed him, or if I just ran into him again, or what, but we ended up hanging out a few times. He was a virgin 'til he was twenty-one, I remember that really well. The seat next to me on the plane was empty so he sat next to me and we talked for the entire six-hour flight. He's living in LA now, he's in a band, and they seem to be doing really well.

I told Toni about it this morning, and his first question was "Did you ever fuck him?"

I was like "No, I never even kissed him."

He was like "Did you blow him?"

I was like "I said I didn't even kiss him."

He was like "But did you blow him and just not kiss him? I know you; you can be sneaky like that."

I love Toni.

October 5

6:00 a.m. Going to see Barry the accountant today to do tax stuff. Nobody better talk to me.

October 6
Paid taxes. Hate watching money leave savings account. So depressed. Not even gonna wear my pedometer today. Nobody better talk to me.

October 7
I talked to the other company again yesterday. So they said they're gonna be able to meet my request, numbers-wise. It would definitely be more work than I'm used to now. But... I need time to finish my book. And the thing is...while they're not technically a gonzo company, they shoot their sex gonzo-style, meaning rougher, less constricted, with the cameramen super close to the action. I hate to say this, but they're marketed toward men, whereas Wicked is marketed toward couples. I resent these kinds of terms because of COURSE there are women (like me, for example!) who prefer to watch gonzo-style porn over feature-style. But it is what it is. As much as I love being at Wicked, it would be a lie to say I didn't sometimes miss fucking gonzo-style.

I don't know. Ugh. I really love being a Wicked girl.

Spiegler goes into surgery in two days. I'm leaving for Lexington, Kentucky, that morning at 6:00 a.m. I hate hate hate that I'm not gonna be here. He keeps telling me there's nothing I can do for him while he's in surgery anyway, and even once he's awake it'll be a while until he can have visitors. I'm already nervous. I'm gonna go see him today.

October 9
Just landed in Lexington, KY. Spiegler is still in surgery.* He should've been out hours ago. I'm a nervous fucking wreck. I cried on the plane in front of my roadie.

*Update: He's out of surgery and the doctor says he is doing great!! He's still in the recovery room so I can't talk to him... BUT YAYY!

October 10

Talked to Spiegler this morning, he is actually sounding really good!

Was a lot more relaxed going to the club last night, knowing Spiegler is okay. This dance gig isn't the best... It's actually my worst one yet. A lot of people in the club, a lot of tips onstage, but when it came time for the signing, like no one bought anything. Hmm. Maybe tonight will be better. We should be done around 4:00 a.m., and then we'll come back to the hotel, pack, and then head to the airport for our 8:00 a.m. flight. I'm gonna go straight to the hospital from LAX.

October 12

I just slept for a full night, but I'm still exhausted. By the time I left the hospital last night, I had been up for forty hours. Good news is Spiegler might actually get released today, in which case I'll go pick him up in a couple of hours! I made him promise me we'll have a Percocet party once he's situated at home. Tee he he he.

October 13

Spiegler didn't get released yesterday, but he gets to go home today at 11:00 a.m.! Last night Jessie Andrews and Lea Lexis came by the hospital, and we all ordered Roscoe's Chicken and Waffles. It was fucking delicious. And then I felt disgusting.

Gonna take Spiegler home in a few hours, and then I'll probably stay and sleep over at his place for at least one or two nights.

I've been thinking...none of this would be possible if I weren't with Wicked. Steve was nice enough to let me get this month off from shooting so that I could take care of Spiegler. I don't think the other company would let me do that.

October 14

I snuck out of Spiegler's house this morning at 6:00 a.m. to go get coffee. Tiptoeing around, shutting the door behind me super quietly and just fast enough so that it doesn't creak...made me feel like a teenager again. It was exhilarating!

I was supposed to meet with the other company today, at their LA office. But yesterday they called me to cancel. I'm not sure if this means they're postponing/rescheduling, or just straight-up canceling the whole thing, or what...

But I've been thinking. I really like my life right now. I love Wicked. There's really no point in leaving. I secretly hope the meeting is just canceled.

October 15
Still at Spiegler's. I had the worst fucking nightmare last night—I usually hate when people tell me about their dreams (unless I'm in them), but this is my diary so I'm gonna fucking talk about it.

THE DREAM

SC.1 INT. ART GALLERY—NIGHT

Camera starts on a close-up of a modern art painting. Pan out, we see TONI male, early forties, and his wife ASA, a much younger, much skinnier female, early twenties, chatting about the art.

                    TONI
        If you look really closely,
        it's like the Catalan flag.

                    ASA
        You say that about everything!

Asa laughs as another couple, MARIA female, mid-thirties, and BOYFRIEND male, mid-thirtiess, approach.

> MARIA
> Oh, this must be the piece she
> was talking about! With the
> flag! The Catalan flag.

Toni notices her right away. This does not escape ASA.

> TONI
> I thought it looked like it.
> Right here, the red is the—

> TONI & MARIA   (together)
> Blood! Jinx!

The two look at each other and smile, clearly enjoying the moment. Asa is jealous.

Camera fades in on Toni's smile.

DISSOLVE TO:

SC. 2 INT. CAR—NIGHT

Asa is sitting in the front passenger's seat, Toni is in the back by himself. We don't see who the driver is; the only thing we do know for certain is that it is one week after the night at the gallery. Asa turns around to face Toni.

                    ASA
        Did you talk to Maria?

                    TONI
        No.

Asa turns back to face the front. But she has a
gut feeling. She turns around again to face Toni.

                    ASA
        Come on. I know you did. Just
        tell me.

Toni sighs, then pauses for a few seconds.

                    TONI
        Okay fine. I did.

Asa turns back around yet again to face the
front. She cries.

                    FIN

I feel like shit now. I've been away from home so much...first, I
was in Kentucky, and now I'm at Spiegler's. And in November,
I'm gone for three weekends out of four.
    I texted him, You're gonna forget about me : (
He replied, Never.
I hope he's right.

October 16
I'm so close to finishing writing the book. The first draft is due

in December, so I've been writing like crazy every morning, even more than the usual two hours. And OF COURSE now that it's crunch time, I discovered a new social media platform. It's called the List App, and I'm fucking obsessed with it.

This is one of the lists I wrote yesterday:

WRITING A BOOK IS...

- 33.3% social media-ing
- 19.2% thinking about writing
- 15% Googling myself
- 11% online shopping
- 8.7% texting
- 6.1% watching gay porn
- 2.5% trying to come up with a title
- 1.7% employing 20/20/20
- 1.5% asking my dog what he's looking at
- 1% writing a book

Obviously, this is an exaggeration. I don't spend nearly 2.5% trying to come up with a title.

October 17

I've seen so many Spiegler girls that I haven't seen in forever in the past week. Bonnie Rotten was here yesterday; she's soooo pregnant and I couldn't stop saying "I can't believe you're growing a human being." She's having a girl.

Do I want a baby? Yes no yes no yes no yes no...I don't know.

Spiegler is doing a lot better overall. He was still really constipated from the medication, so this morning I gave him some Milk of Magnesia. He's been in the bathroom for over an hour now. Success?

October 19

I went home for two hours yesterday. Toni is the best. He's been taking care of Homie by himself this whole week, and hasn't once asked me anything like "Are you coming home yet?"

He knows how much Spiegler means to me.

October 20

Not so much to say these days... I'm still at Spiegler's. It's been a very nice routine since I've been here.

6:30 a.m.: Wake up, sneak out quietly so I don't wake Spiegler up, go to Starbucks because there is no coffee machine here. Scream at traffic the entire 0.5 miles there, buy coffee, drink ONE SIP ONLY, drive the 0.5 miles back a little more calmly.

7:00 a.m.: Write write write write.

Noon: Spiegler wakes up, eats something, goes for a walk with his walker up and down the hall once. This pains his back, so I give him half a painkiller. Watch TV until Spiegler falls asleep from pain meds.

2:00 p.m.: Go back to writing.

4:00 p.m.: Spiegler wakes up again. Usually around this time, someone visits. Eat. Hang out.

6:00 p.m.: Try to get Spiegler to take a laxative. Argue. Hang out.

7:00 p.m.: Time for another walk up and down the hallway and another half of a painkiller. Another mini-nap.

8:30 p.m.: Spiegler wakes up again. Maybe eats something. We watch TV or a movie together.

11:00 p.m.: Go to bed.

October 21
I think I might go home today—I don't think Spiegler needs me here overnight anymore. Toni said Homie peed on the floor a couple of times because he's mad that I'm not home. Aww : (

October 22
Came home last night. Gonna go back to Spiegler's today after boot camp. I haven't worked out in two weeks. I feel really disgusting. I'm shooting a gangbang in less than two weeks (my first one ever for Wicked, possibly the first one Wicked has ever shot. I'll have to look into it), and I wanna be in the best shape possible. The move is kind of a promo for my RealDoll, so I need to at least be somewhat as skinny as my doll.

Also in this movie: Stormy Daniels and jessica drake are gonna fuck. Actually, all three Wicked girls are doing a three-way. This'll be the first time we three are fucking, and the first time Stormy and jessica do a scene together in over TEN years. I'm really nervous. Is it gonna be awkward? Is it gonna be crazy passionate? I already told jessica that if she and Stormy get so wound up that they totally leave me out, I'll completely under-stand, and go on asshole-licking duty.

October 25
Talked to someone at the other company today. I asked if our meeting was canceled, and they answered yes. I'm actually glad. I'm glad they made the offer; it made me realize that I really like my life right now. I love the company I'm with. I'm so lucky.

Haiku

How rude that you'd think
That I would pee in your pool
I was just squirting

Narnia

New York City was supposed to be the city that never slept. Yet, here I was at 11:00 p.m. flipping channels on the small television in my room. Where was everybody? Jules and his girlfriend Sia were in bed, with work the next morning. Pete was hooking up with some guy from the bar at his apartment, an event I was not invited to. My cousin was home with her husband and baby, spending quality family time. I had already spent the maximum time possible with my parents, staying two nights and three days at their loft. Anything more than that, and I would go crazy. This was not an exaggeration, but a scientifically proven fact, backed by years of research, sweat, and tears.

Repeatedly pushing the channel button, I sighed. Not so long ago, 11:00 p.m. was still hours away from bedtime—11:00pm was when my friends and I would leave the house. The fact that it was a weekday made no difference. To show up anywhere before midnight was considered lame—did the times change, or did we? Were we really that old? In LA, I was a working wife, I had no friends or social life—and I was okay with that. But NYC? The city wasn't supposed to change on me. It was where I returned to remember where I came from, to remember how cool I once was. It was where I hit no less than three spots a night, ate dinner at 4:00 a.m., and retired to bed once the sun was already up.

Having spent all day cooped up in my room writing, high on caffeine, I was now stir crazy and in need of a change of scenery. I always did this—once focused on something, I was unable to step away or enjoy anything else. It's like the opposite of ADD.

I threw the remote off the bed and stretched my body out. I had hardly moved from the one spot all day, leaving my neck and back in pain. Rolling over, I opened my computer, and typed "24-hour massage NYC" into the search bar. In the midst of shady Craigslist links and ads for Asian Happy Ending Happy Price Flushing, Queens, I found a Yelp review of a place that had an average of three-and-a-half stars from twenty-one reviews. Not great, but I couldn't expect much at that hour. The price was a little high, but the reviews convinced me it would be worth it— the main draw being that they were mostly written by women. The last thing I needed right then was to waltz into a rub-and-tug, only to have my request for a deep tissue massage rejected— or worse, accepted and delivered poorly from a non-masseuse who would rather be giving a handjob for a a bigger tip. Just to be sure, I clicked on the link to their website. Sure enough, there it was in the FAQ:

```
Do you offer "tantric/sensual" massage?

We absolutely do not offer tantric or sensual
massage. We only provide professional, ther-
apeutic massage by New York State Licensed
Massage   Therapists.   Any   suggestion   of
this nature and you will be escorted out.
```

I made an appointment for 12:30 a.m., which I figured would give me enough time to get there and enjoy the steam room and sauna for half an hour before my massage. Riding the elevator down, I briefly considered walking over the Brooklyn Bridge into Manhattan. I'm not sure if it was a newfound maturity-induced logic, or if living in LA for so long had turned me soft, but I quickly decided it would be dangerous, and hailed a cab.

A year before, I would never have considered staying at a hotel in Brooklyn. Although my parents moved off the island years ago, I grew up in Manhattan. Everyone I knew lived in Manhattan. My whole social life had always been in Manhattan. Even as that slowly shifted, and everyone migrated to the other side of the East River, I stubbornly stayed at the more expensive hotels in Manhattan, taking cabs every day over the bridge to see my friends. This current trip was the first one home when I realized that it was time to give in—Manhattan was officially an island none of my friends could afford to live on.

Growing up, I was certain that if I were to have kids, it was imperative that they grow up in the city. New York kids were smarter, quicker, and funnier—I looked down on kids from anywhere else. They were somehow corny in my eyes, sheltered and naïve. I grew up with kids of all colors, whose parents came from all walks of life. I was privileged enough to attend a Manhattan private school, which I now realize is practically the equivalent of a liberal arts college education. I had friends who were wealthy, who taught me culture and class—and I had friends from the projects, who showed me street smarts. While kids in most places relied on their parents to drive them everywhere they went, we were free to roam the city on our own as soon as we could read a subway map. We were lying to our parents, sneaking off by train to three-day raves in New Jersey by the time we were in middle school—something that would be impossible almost anywhere else in the country. A good fake ID was easy to get, and even if you didn't have one, there was always a bodega around the corner that would sell you almost anything you wanted. As a result, my friends and I grew up faster than most.

Looking back now, I'm frightened for myself as a youth. There were so many opportunities for me to be raped, murdered, or even just overdose and die. I can't believe I took the G train alone at four in the morning, high on acid, practically inviting people to come rape me. While my teenaged self was so sure my own children would grow up in the city, my thirty-year old self shuddered at the idea of raising a child in such an uncontrollable environment.

When the cab pulled up to the curb, I looked around and started to doubt my web-based judgment—I scolded myself for not knowing better. I had been on this street numerous times, mostly to visit karaoke bars after a night of partying, and had never seen anything that remotely resembled a legitimate spa. This time was no different.

I found the building, and got into the elevator. It was in no way inviting, much less zen—old and rusty, it creaked as it slowly took me up to the fifth floor. Had I just made a big mistake? What was I about to get myself into?

Contrary to my concerns, the doors opened to something quite unexpected. Classical music was playing, and the spa entrance was beautiful—tranquil even. It was as if I had walked through a closet door into Narnia. Coming from the urine-covered streets of New York, through a rickety elevator the size of a small pantry, even colors looked different here.

A young blonde woman greeted me from behind the desk.

"Hi there," she warmly smiled. "Do you have the appointment at twelve-thirty?"

"Yes," I smiled back, "This place is so nice! I was getting a little worried in the elevator."

"A lot of our first-time clients say that," she laughed. "Now it's Asa, right? Am I pronouncing that correctly?"

"Yes," I replied. "You pronounced it perfectly." My whole life, this was something I struggled with. Ass-a, Ay-sa, Asia—at least ninety percent of the time, my name was pronounced wrong. And who could blame them? Even in Japan, my name is not a regular one. Since I was a young child, I swore that if I ever had kids, they would have normal, easy-to-pronounce names.

To my envy, the woman introduced herself as Sarah, and asked me if I had brought a swimming suit. I hadn't.

"No worries." She bent down and grabbed what looked like some tissue paper, and placed it on top of a robe. "You can wear the disposable one we provide."

I looked at the tissue paper once again, and realized that it was a disposable bikini. "Can I go naked?" I asked.

"I'm sorry, we require all clients to cover up in the public area of the spa. Of course in the massage room, you can go nude if you'd be more comfortable," she explained.

I nodded my head, and she handed me the robe and bikini before leading me to my locker. "Once you're changed, just walk through those doors," she pointed past the showers, "and I'll give you a tour."

The locker room was empty, and like the entrance, clean and pretty. Having worn a sweatsuit and no makeup there, it took me hardly any time to get changed. I looked at myself in the paper bikini and made a mental note to bring my own swimsuit the next time. It was clearly a "one-size-fits-all" deal, which, as I knew from years of buying stripper outfits, almost always meant "one-size-fits-nobody." The top was baggy even on my fake C cups, and the bottoms looked like adult diapers, coming up above my navel. I used my phone to take a photo in the mirror, and sent it to Toni, laughing on the inside, remembering that these goofy photos I sent him throughout the day had once been sexy ones. I made another mental note, this time to send him a photo he might actually find attractive once I was back at the hotel.

After adjusting the bikini, rolling it down to look as normal as possible, I stepped through the doors into the spa. My eyes immediately went to a couple who were sitting in one of the Jacuzzis with glasses of champagne, and I noticed they had brought their own swimming suits. The spa was gorgeous—everything made of stone, and stations of cucumber, pineapple, and orange water were placed every few feet. Sarah showed me around the Jacuzzis and various rooms, and I quickly settled into the empty sauna. It seemed the couple in the Jacuzzi were the only other people here, and I laid down and enjoyed the silence.

Silence was something I'd always been good at. As an only child, it was my default mode. Sitting in a room with nothing, staring at a blank wall, left with nothing but my imagination was something I'd always been able to do for hours. It was a great thing, knowing if I ever became homeless, I could probably excel as a nun or prisoner.

When it was time, my masseuse came to get me. I was relieved to see she was Asian—Sarah from the front desk had me secretly worried. It wasn't a racist thing, just a fact—old Asian ladies gave the strongest massages.

As she rubbed my body, I realized I had not been massaged for over a month. Back home in LA, a massage was a treat I usually indulged in at least once every two weeks. There was always, without fail, a moment in the session when I was convinced that my masseuse wanted to fuck me—it didn't matter if she was a non-English speaking Vietnamese lady who could have easily been my grandmother. There always came a point, usually when she was somewhere near my thighs, when I was fully convinced we were only a matter of seconds away from her touching my vagina. Of course, this never happened, and I always walked out of the spa feeling like a fool for once again imagining such a thing.

Such was the case this time. As she sat me up and hit my back one last time with her fist signaling the end of our session, I once again felt like an idiot.

Walking back out into the public area of the spa, for a second I considered going back to the sauna—but decided against it, as it was already two-thirty in the morning. I entered the locker room, to find a girl getting undressed. As she removed her top, I saw that she had the one of the worst tit jobs I had ever seen, which was saying a lot, considering I lived in LA.

"Did you just get a massage?" she asked, catching me by surprise. I hoped she had not seen me staring at her botched surgery. "I just love this place." Her eyes were half open, and I realized this girl was definitely high on something, something that looked like something I would love. She probably didn't notice me looking.

"Yeah," I answered. "It's my first time here, this place is amazing. And it's twenty-four-hours, I love that."

"I come here a lot," she slowly slurred. "I'm Kiki." She stuck out her hand for me to shake, and I quickly assessed the situation. She had fake tits. She was comfortable shaking my hand while topless. She was high. And her name was Kiki. This was getting interesting.

"Nice to meet you, I'm Asa." I took her hand.

"Are you here alone?" She asked. I nodded my head. "I'm here on a date," she said, eyes almost closed, and took three full seconds to form a smile. I immediately wondered what kind of date she meant. I hated to stereotype, but this girl was definitely at least a stripper.

Just then, two more girls came walking in. They were dressed in short bright-colored dresses and carried expensive purses.

"Hi ladies," the one in yellow sang, in a voice probably too loud for a spa. She turned back around to her friend in neon pink. "So I told him I'm a businesswoman—I don't play those games."

I opened my locker and tried to hide my excitement as I continued to eavesdrop. I unwrapped my towel.

"So anyway—are we meeting those guys for dinner tomorrow or what? I was gonna..." The yellow one stopped mid-sentence and looked at me. "Damn girl, I like your breasts! Are they real?"

I shook my head. "I went to Dr. Hidalgo on Park Ave. He's the best," I smiled.

"I'm Mercedes." She held out her hand. "And this is Nikki," she nodded toward her pink friend. Again, I didn't want to stereotype, but their names were Mercedes and Nikki. And they were in short, neon dresses.

"I'm Asa," I introduced myself again. I looked toward Kiki, who was paying no attention. She was now wearing a thong bikini. Something about this surprised me—somehow, a thong bikini felt more obscene than actual nudity, especially for a spa.

"Kiki?" Mercedes asked when she saw her. "Girl I didn't even recognize you!"

Kiki laughed. "I'm on a date. Like a real one. He's a lawyer."

Like a real one. She had said the words I needed to hear. These girls were hookers. For the second time that night, I felt like one of the Narnia kids.

Right then, I decided that 2:30 a.m. wasn't so late after all. I sat down on the bench in front of my locker.

"He's so hot, here let me show you a picture," Kiki continued, taking out her phone. She was speaking so slowly, it was almost painful—it reminded me of the days when I used to do opiates and I thought I was acting so natural.

As if she were reading my mind, Mercedes laughed, "Girl you are high as fuck. Speaking of which, do you think I can party in here?" She took out a baggie with white powder.

"No girl, you don't wanna do that here, are you crazy?" Kiki slurred. I thought she was talking about the locker room, when she continued, "You're here to relax. You want the opposite of that. That stuff's gonna make you all hyper." I realized she was suggesting that Mercedes not do *coke* here. Not: not do coke *here*.

"Don't worry, this stuff doesn't affect me like that." Mercedes looked offended. "I'm just asking if it's safe to do here."

"Better in here than out there," Kiki replied. I didn't know if she meant out there, the spa, or out there, the streets. This was like decoding another language, a wonderful, beautiful hooker language.

Mercedes turned to me. "You party?" I took a second to try to understand what she was asking. Usually, when someone asked if you partied, it meant they were asking if you did drugs. But here, I wasn't so sure—was she asking me if I hooked? I thought about it, and then realized it didn't matter—the answer to both was the same.

"No, but thanks," I politely smiled. "Do you guys come here a lot?" I decided I wanted these girls to be my best friends for the rest of my spa visit.

"A lot of the girls come here, but I've only been here a couple of times," Mercedes answered. "Are you from here?"

"I grew up here," I answered. "But I live in LA now. This is my first time here—" I paused and realized I didn't want her to think I was judgmental, or worse, a prude. "I do porn," I said as casually as I could, in my best *I'm one of you* voices. I immediately felt corny, like a mom trying to bond with her hip, teenaged daughter.

Both the other girls, who had been rummaging through their lockers, turned around to look at me.

"Euw."

"Why?"

The girls were clearly not impressed. Not in a good way, anyway. A moment ago, their guards had been down, talking about dates this and drugs that. In a matter of seconds, it was as if an invisible shield had gone up, separating *me* from *them*.

"I like it," I smiled as friendly as I could. "I've always wanted to do it. I know it sounds weird, but it's just always been my dream."

"You *want* to do porn?" Nikki, who had previously been silent, asked. "Girl, that's crazy."

Nervous and not knowing how else to react, I laughed. Were these girls actually *judging* me? Weren't we all in the same sex-for-money boat? "I know, it's crazy to most people," I tried to reason. "But I just love it."

The girls each turned around and went back to changing, not saying another word. As they silently left the locker room, I heard them burst out into laughter as soon as the doors closed behind them.

"Cunts," I murmured under my breath. They were the ones talking about heroin versus cocaine in a spa, and *I* was the laughable one? And I had just been looking forward to spending an extra hour or two here, chatting it up with them. Maybe, if things had gone well, we could even have gone to brunch the next day. I quickly got dressed and left the locker room, to find a man arguing with Sarah at the front desk.

"Why do I have to give you all this information?" he asked, holding a clipboard. "I'm paying everything upfront." He looked up at me as I walked out, and I could tell he knew who I was. For the final time that night, I stereotyped: middle-aged white guy getting a massage at 3:00 a.m., and knows who I am—he must be here for a "date." I rushed out before he could ask me any questions.

When I got back to the hotel, I got back on my computer and pulled up the spa's website. Regardless of how the hookers had *Mean Girl*-ed me, I had discovered something magical—it was something I needed to know everything about. Was this a happy-ending place? Was it somewhere hookers took their johns? Was it somewhere hookers *met* their johns? Or was it someplace they just came to relax after their shifts? Scrolling through the website, I felt like a moron—it was so obvious now. There were services listed like this:

GYNO SPA CURE: Try this ancient remedy that Asian cultures have known for centuries. Utilizing healing herbs to irrigate the vaginal passage to restore optimum health.

And FAQs like this:

Who comes there during the late-night hours? Our most frequent clients are performers and dancers who finish their shows after 11:00 p.m. and have been on their feet all day. We provide a place for them to relax and receive treatments.

And there on the front page, was this:

The spa opens its doors for couples every evening from 5:00 p.m. to 7:00 a.m.

Of course. The signs were all there, I just hadn't looked hard enough. I was usually so good at spotting shady things—too good, even. I often projected my own perverted thoughts and saw every laundromat as a front for a prostitution ring in the basement.

Smiling, I crawled under the covers. Those hooker bitches had thought I was so gross. What an absolutely dream-like night! And at 5:00 a.m., I finally went to sleep in the city that never sleeps.

Haiku

I just don't get why
You'd use your hand when you could
Use your vagina

Coming Out

As a teenager, I often fantasized that I would one day have a gay best friend. The way many young girls dream about their future husbands coming to sweep them off their feet, I would build castles in the air about meeting my gay best friend—it would be a moment full of "Girl, where have you been all my life?" and "Oh my god, me too!" We would have sleepovers where we watched girly movies, browsed through catalogues, and talked shit about the other girls in our grade. It might seem like I'm generalizing that one, I think all gay men are basically me, only with a penis; or two, I'm fetishizing, as though anyone would suffice as long as they were male, gay, and flamboyant. At the time, both things were probably true. Growing up, my mother had a gay best friend; my favorite television characters had gay best friends; and being from New York City, it seemed that everyone had a gay best friend. It felt to me as if life as a female would be incomplete without one. But as the years went by, and I graduated high school and eventually left the city, it seemed that special guy would never enter my life.

Fast-forward to when I was twenty-two. I was sitting on a stoop in SoHo with Peter, whom I hadn't seen in a few months. For the past year, I had been living in Florida, stripping, being the "Show Whore" (official title) on a radio show whose target audience consisted of self-proclaimed redneck truckers—I was just living the glamorous life, really. Peter was always the first person I called when I visited home—we had been friends since we were thirteen or fourteen. He was the younger brother of my then-boyfriend's best friend Jules, and we had spent countless nights in his bedroom secretly doing drugs together, promising each other we wouldn't tell his brother. Eventually, my ex and I broke up, but Peter and I remained close. He was my most handsome friend, but we'd never had sex—it had always been clear there was no sexual tension between us. This was a boy who wore long johns in front of me when I slept over—like I said, zero sexual tension.

"Have you been hooking up with anyone?" I asked as usual, as we shared a cigarette.

"Well, actually," Peter said turning to face me. "I'm gay."

I nearly fell off the stoop. Of all the happy moments in my life, this was in the top five. I took a moment to make sure this was reality, and then punched Peter in the arm. "Shut the fuck up!"

I was beaming.

"It's true," Peter said matter of factly.

"How long have you known?"

"I think I *always* kind of knew."

"What kind of guys are you into?"

"Honestly? I like guys that kind of look like me."

We laughed. What a perfect answer!

"I'm so happy for you! Who else knows?" As I drilled him with questions, Peter calmly answered them all. So far he had told one of his brothers, but most of the people in his life, including his parents, had yet to know. He had been meeting up with some guys he met online, and he had started to frequent gay bars. He wasn't completely decided on where he stood on the Kinsey Scale of sexuality, but there it was, just as I had imagined, our first *Oh my god, me too!*

"All along, you were right in front of me," I told him.

That summer, I watched Peter slowly come out to everyone in his life. He had his first serious boyfriend; he had his heart broken for the first time. I'd never been more proud of someone; coming from a family that consisted of a conservative Egyptian/British mother, a Polish veteran father, and two masculine brothers, it couldn't have been easy. I saw a sense of confidence grow in him that had never been there before.

Fast-forward again a little over a year to when I started porn. I had some coming-out of my own to do—although my friends knew I was showing off my inner organs on the Internet, my parents did not. And as close as I was with my family, I had no desire to tell them. "Why taint the relationship? They're just going to be upset by it. Besides, maybe they'll never find out. I'm willing to take that chance," I'd tell people. But less than six months into my new career, my mother called me to tell me the bad news.

"We saw something on the television," she said gravely over the phone.

I didn't ask for details, and instead stayed silent.

"What did I do wrong? Why are you doing this?" she cried over and over.

I had no answer.

What followed was two years of a very strained maternal relationship. While we still talked constantly, conversations ended in arguments more often than not. My father wasn't as affected—he asked me if I was happy, I answered yes, and that was pretty much it. But my mother...she needed to understand *Why? What happened to you that you want to have sex for money?* It was something I could only answer with "I need to do porn or I'll regret it forever," which made things even more confusing for her.

For my mother, who had likely lost her virginity to my father, it was unfathomable that I was doing this for my own sake.

While I don't regret my decision of entering a career my mother was less than enthusiastic about, I regret letting my fear of confrontation affect our relationship—looking back, I wish I had had control of how she had found out her daughter was doing porn. I'm still unsure exactly what she saw, whether it was me fully clothed in an interview, or just full-on fucking and sucking a guy's dick while another pounded my pussy. If I had just been straight up with her, if I had told her, rather than deceiving her for those six months, maybe it would have been easier for her to accept.

It's been eight years now, and my mother and I are once again back to the happy relationship we had before I did porn. We still don't talk about my job in detail, but it's something she's come to accept. I don't think there was ever a specific turning point or an "aha" moment when she finally understood me—I think she just slowly learned to live with it. At this point, I think she is confident that if this isn't what made me happy, I wouldn't be doing it. She sees that I am healthy, happy, and responsible. I've been recognized by fans a few times while we've been in public together, and though she seemed uncomfortable at first, she laughs it off now. We are slowly able to talk about things more—before, I never mentioned words like "work" or "job," but now I can casually tell my mom, "I'll call you back, I'm shooting." It may not seem like much, but this is huge progress. It's still a process, and in a way, I think I'm still coming out. When my first book was published, I specifically asked her not to read it—but I think one day when she's ready, she will. In it, I included a letter to her. It was the letter I wish I could have written to her when I started porn.

It pains me that I have a huge area of my life I cannot share with my mother—we have always talked about everything, analyzing things together, for the sake of, well, just sharing everything. We do, again, now—but just not about porn. On a good day, I justify this by reminding myself that most daughters do not share their sex lives with their parents; it just so happens that my sex life is my job. On a bad day, I wonder if the decision I've made is heartless beyond apology.

I envy Peter and the confidence and smoothness he chose to come out with. While his sexual orientation and my choice of career are not the same thing, we both had an aspect of ourselves we were nervous to share with our loved ones. If only I had done the same as he did and delivered my news personally, I wouldn't have lost those two years with my mother; I wouldn't still be in the process of coming out at age thirty.

Although he's younger than me, I look up to Peter. He's not the showy, flamboyant gay best friend I had once dreamt of as a teenager; he's way better.

HAIKU

Dead bug in my drink
Eh, whatever, cause I have
Swallowed worse before

Undecided

Another year of wasted eggs because I chose to whore instead.

"Do you wanna hold him?"

I did. I wanted to hold him and squeeze him and kiss his tiny peanut forehead and pretend it was I who had given birth. I wanted to softly swing him side to side in my arms, like I had done as a child with my Cabbage Patch dolls. I wanted to put my nipple in his mouth and see if he would latch on with his perfect little lips, as he looked up at me, silently thanking me with his eyes for giving him life, love, and food.

But I was scared.

The reality was that I had never held a baby. It looked easy enough, until I had the opportunity to do it.

Maya must have seen the nerves on my face. "Just hold him. You're not gonna drop him." Smiling, she held him out to me, one hand under his head, the other under his body. I positioned my arms into a cradle and thought how bizarre this moment was.

At twenty-seven, Maya was my first friend to pass on an abortion. It seemed that while the rest of the country had been starting families and getting fat for the last half decade, the two coasts were busy making careers, experimenting with drugs and online dating, not yet ready to stop being selfish. When she first told me on the phone she was pregnant, my response had been not congratulatory excitement, but sympathetic apology.

"Oh shit, that sucks. I'm so sorry. Do you know whose it is? How far along are you? Do you feel like shit?"

"This Brazilian guy I met in Japan. It's been three months. I'm throwing up every day."

It wasn't until I asked if she needed a recommendation for a clinic that I realized she was planning on keeping it.

I flew back to New York and saw Maya a few times throughout her pregnancy. We had known each other since we were two years old, when our mothers enrolled us in a Saturday Japanese School in order for us to have some sense of our culture. Both of us being only children of Japanese immigrants in New York City, we saw each other more as family than friends, and we often pretended to strangers that we were twins. To this day I refer to her as my cousin, and her parents are my auntie and uncle.

As I saw her belly grow with each trip to the city, I couldn't quite believe she was going to be a mother. I was ready for her to give up at any second, go in for a late-term abortion, or maybe even reveal it had all been a joke—anything would be more believable than Maya having a baby. Even as I touched her stomach and felt the little legs kicking against my hand, I didn't think this thing in her stomach would ever become an actual being. This was a girl I had done drugs with since age thirteen. We had shoplifted together. We had snuck out of our houses and gone boy-hunting at 3:00 a.m. together. We had spent hours constructing elaborate lies to tell our parents. And now—now, she was going to *be* a parent. This kid's first word was going to be "Fuck."

As a child, I was extremely drawn to pregnancy: my preschool teacher, Maria from *Sesame Street*, that girl from *Degrassi Junior High*. In kindergarten, my friend Sally had a photo on her fridge of when her mother was pregnant with her. I used to stare at that photo whenever I went over for a play date, using any excuse I could to go to the kitchen once more. I'd trace my fingers over the bump, and when I got home, I would go to my room and touch myself, imagining her announcing to me over and over, "I'm pregnant."

I don't know where the fascination came from, or why it made me horny. At the time, I didn't identify the feeling, or even masturbating, as sexual—but looking back, it was definitely horniness I was feeling. I had not yet learned how babies were made, but maybe it's the kind of knowledge that's ingrained in us on some sort of a primal level—at least, this is what I've told myself to make it less weird. Even now, nothing turns me on more than when Toni cums inside of me. When he starts picking up the pace, and makes that face he only does when he's about to cum, it makes me orgasm instantly.

"Cum inside me, make me pregnant!" I'll yell, right before we orgasm at the same time, which is ridiculous, considering I've been on birth control since I was fifteen.

Aside from getting cream-pied, though, I hadn't given pregnancy much thought as an adult. So when Maya got knocked up, my questions were more scientific.

"Are you afraid you'll get fat?"

She'd shrug and answer, "I haven't even had time to think about it." As shocking as the reply was, I believed it.

Her answer remained the same once Kai was born. "Honestly I don't even care. My whole life is different now—it revolves around him," she'd tell me on the phone.

I was desperately jealous. A life without the fear of weight gain was unfathomable to me. I wanted to feel that—I wanted to know what it was to have something so important that it didn't even matter if I got fat.

"Maybe I should have a baby," I'd think as I hung up.

Then I'd drive to my set for the day—a double penetration scene—and imagine myself going home later that evening with cum in my hair from two men who were not my husband, who were not the father of my imaginary baby.

I'd decide I was not yet ready.

"See? You're fine!" Maya encouragingly smiled, patting Kai's head as I held him. He was heavier than I had anticipated—probably because Maya had insisted how light he would be for my Barry's boot camp-trained arms. I sat frozen, scared to stand, move, or even breathe. I wondered if it was possible that I looked at all natural holding this little person in my arms.

"Where's your phone? I gotta take a picture of this." Maya clapped her hands together.

"Over there," I nodded toward my purse.

As Maya took the photo of us, I felt guilt hit me the way an ecstasy tab does—inching closer and closer, so slowly you weren't sure if you were just imagining it—until it finally just encompassed you in an undeniable way. I didn't deserve to be in this photo. I didn't deserve to hold this little human. Only three days ago, I had been sitting in something called a blowjob cage. What if Kai looked back on this picture one day and felt disgust? What if someone found this photo and thought it was part of a porno? What if this kid grew up to be a politician? If this picture surfaced, his chances would be over. I let Maya take the photo on my phone, but swore to myself I would delete it as soon as I left.

I spent the rest of the afternoon watching Maya be a mother. Kai would go in and out of naps as she folded his tiny little laundry, breastfed him, and burped him afterward. She looked so natural, as if she were a whole new person—she was so *good* at being a mother. Not for one moment did she look how I felt when I had held Kai. I tried to imagine myself doing the same things. There were moments I could, but there were more moments I could not.

I flew home to LA sure I would never bear a child. It was too late for me. I had done too much. Not only had I fucked too many people, but too many people had seen me fucking too many people. It wasn't something I regretted—but I supposed this is what they meant when they said you couldn't have it all. It saddened me. The same way I knew if I had never done porn, I would've forever looked back and regretted it, I knew that if I never had a child, I wouldn't feel fulfilled in life. I pulled out my phone and looked at the photo of me and Kai. As my finger hovered over the "delete" button, another feeling hit me like an ecstasy tab—only this time, the feeling was hope. I let my finger back away, so slowly I wasn't even sure if it was moving. Finally, I told myself I didn't have to delete the picture right away—I could keep it for myself for now and make that decision later.

HAIKU

Behind sunglasses
I creep on your camel toe
And pretend to sleep

The first time I ever had a girl-on-girl interaction was during the summer vacation in between ninth and tenth grades. It wasn't so much vacation for me, since I was once again in summer school. It had been a couple of years since I had discovered sex, drugs, and, well, just sex and drugs, and I had been ordered to attend summer school if I wanted to avoid being held back a year.

The girls I messed around with were Nica and Piper. They both went to La Guardia, a public school for the arts, and we had been hanging out all summer. It was somewhat planned—more so than any time I had fucked a guy, anyway. We were with a group of ten or so other kids at a movie premiere. Which sounds fancier than it actually is—when you're in high school in NYC, you do things like this. It's normal. I don't remember what the movie was, but I do remember we sat behind the members of N'Sync. This was before Justin Timberlake got hot, when his hair still looked like precooked Cup-a-Noodle.

"We should hook up tonight," Nica whispered in my ear as we were all walking to the theatre. "With Piper. I've never had a threesome."

"Me neither."

And so it was decided. I've always been easy.

After finding our seats, the three of us went to the bathroom, went into a stall together, and proceeded to make out and take turns rubbing each other's clits. None of us came, but orgasming wasn't so important back then. Once we had each had a turn, we went back to our seats and told everyone.

I've had many gay experiences since then, and I've gotten a lot better at it. But while I love fucking women, I don't consider myself a lesbian. If I were to be in a relationship with a woman, I'd pick the kind who looks like a boy—Ruby Rose from *Orange is the New Black* and Shane from *The L Word* come to mind. Maybe this just means I'm straight. Is there a label for a woman who likes sex with women as much as sex with men, but when it comes to relationships, she is only interested in men? If so, I'd like to know, because it would save me a lot of time when explaining my sexuality.

There's a term going around among kids these days (now that I'm thirty, I feel I can say things like this): WCW. Not to be mistaken with WCW: World Championship Wrestling, or WCWS: Worst-Case Wife Scenario. I'm talking about WCW: Woman Crush Wednesday. WCW is usually announced on social media in the form of a hashtag, followed by the name of the woman you are crushing on that week.

In no particular order, these are my #WCWs:

JESSICA DRAKE

jessica prefers that her name be written in all lowercase. She's been contracted to Wicked for most of her career, and she has never shot a scene without a condom. She spends her free time volunteering for various charities, and once a year, she goes to a third-world country to build houses. She's gorgeous, blonde, and naturally skinny; she cooks, she cleans, she's smart, she's funny, she is a great conversationalist, and she is equally bisexual. Despite everything I just said in this paragraph, I initially assumed she was an evil bitch.

Over the seven years I've known her, I've come to find that she is, in fact, genuinely the nicest and most impeccable woman I've ever met—her spotless image is not just an image. I keep waiting for her to slip up—for her to reveal her true nasty self. But the reality is that she just really is that kind. We've become close, and she was the biggest campaigner for me in getting my Wicked contract. I've since learned things about her past, and I see why she is so empathetic. Despite my natural inclination to hate perfect people, she has won me over.

The first time we fucked was for a movie creatively named *Sex*, shot right before I signed with Wicked. I was not looking forward to the scene. jessica is the type of hottie that people assume get by on their looks. Her body *and* face are both the universal ideal, which is something I generally find both unfair and suspicious. I assumed she would just "phone it in," just go through the sex positions and make no real connection with me.

Once again, jessica proved me wrong. She fucked me so passionately that at one point in the scene, the director had to inform us we were no longer on the set—we had somehow ended up on the floor twenty feet away from the desk we were supposed to be fucking on. She was dirty, she hit me when I liked, and she invited me to hit her when she liked. She submitted to me just as much as she demanded I submit to her. She ate my pussy and made me cum even when the cameras were not rolling. Not once did she yell "cut" to get her makeup touched up, which was something I had expected to happen at least twice. It was one of my favorite lesbian scenes I'd ever shot.

Now, I request to work with jessica every chance I get. She is one of the few people in the world I seek out for advice in every area of life. She is humble despite the fact that she does not need to be, and she is not at all pretentious, when she totally could be. I look up to her in a way I don't to most people. I aspire to be as good as her, fully knowing I never will.

Whenever I come to an ethical crossroads, I think to myself: WWjD? What Would jessica Do?

STORMY DANIELS

The easiest way for me to start my love letter to Stormy is by showing you my diary entry from the day I worked with her for the first time.

December 4th

Let me start by saying how much I hate when people use the word "epic" to describe things that are not. Okay, now let me tell you how epic today was.

I did a lesbian scene with Stormy Daniels. She's one of the few porn stars I really knew about before entering the industry, so that alone is pretty great.

When I signed with Wicked (one year ago), she started putting me in her movies, I'd say pretty much one every two months. But here's the thing—she only booked me to fuck other people, but never herself! When a director does this, it's pretty obvious it means they don't want to fuck you, so I was pretty bummed out. I figured I wasn't her type or whatever, which I understand, I can't be everyone's flavor, but it kind of hurt my feelings because I really wanted to fuck her.

AND THEN LAST MONTH SHE BOOKED ME FOR THIS MOVIE AND WHEN I LOOKED AT THE CALL SHEET, MY SCENE PARTNER WAS HER!

Okay, now that that's out of the way, let me say that everything I love about Stormy is on the opposite end of the spectrum as jessica.

Stormy IS an evil bitch. She is mean, she yells at people, and as a director, she is known to make people cry on her sets. Her hotness matches her personality completely. "Resting bitch face" is a phrase she probably inspired. The first time I shot for her, she played a prank on me, yelling at my male costar and kicking him off the set, instilling a fear in me that to this day has not left. One time, she made me audition for a movie on tape, made me gallop around the room on a stick horse in the nude in front of the entire crew, before revealing that I was not even being considered for the part in the first place. She continuously writes parts for me that involve things I'm terrified of, including hanging me upside down from the ceiling by a tiny piece of rope. This is her sense of humor. If I tell her I hate her, she considers her day a success.

Secretly, though, deep down, Stormy is kind. She is an amazing mother and is raising a truly good kid. She loves her animals and will go the ends of the earth to take care of them. She told me once, "I suck dick to feed my horses," and she was serious. She is fiercely loyal to her film crew in a way that's very rare to see. I know she defends me when people say something mean about me behind my back, because I've heard it from multiple people who have witnessed it.

I think she would hate to know that I know.

For all these reasons, I love her. She is the kind of mean that I work best under, she keeps me on my best behavior, and she rewards me with tiny moments of niceness when I am good, before immediately returning to her usual ice-queen self. She makes me understand why people get Stockholm syndrome.

She is true to who she is regardless of the situation. She will never be nice just for the sake of keeping the peace. She is one of the strongest alpha females I have ever met, but if I ever told her that, she'd probably yell at me for reducing her to her gender stereotype.

DANA DEARMOND

Dana is a fellow Spiegler girl. She is THE Spiegler girl. On Spiegler's website, there are five rows of girls on the front page—the goal is to be on the top row. Spiegler will forever claim that there is no order to the rows, that being on the top row doesn't necessarily mean anything, but we all know that is bullshit. Dana is the first person on the top row. I am the second. I always joke that I will never be number one, because Dana will never retire.

If the Spiegler girls were a sorority, Dana would be president. If we were hookers, she'd be bottom bitch. If we were the cast of *Mean Girls*, she'd be Regina George.

The first time I met her was at a Fourth of July party, a few weeks after I had gotten into porn. She was sitting at a table with the rest of the Spiegler girls. Loudly boasting about her anal capabilities, she was obviously the ringleader. This was before I had ever shot anal, before I had done pretty much anything. I was highly intimidated.

Eight years later, I am her number-one fan, and although she has yet to profess it publicly as I do so often, I think she is mine. I'm her Gretchen Weiner. I like to think we are two of the funniest people in porn, but I know for a fact she *is* the funniest. When I'm with her, my ab muscles get a workout because she makes me laugh so much. She likes for people to think she's a hardass bitch, but in reality, she is a sensitive crybaby. One time she saw a guy fail in a scene (he couldn't get it up), and she cried because she felt bad for him.

Haiku

Aside from gangbangs
Group text is my preferred form
Of socializing

Domino

"You know what I never seen in a porno before?"

"Hmm?" I replied from the backseat, scrolling through my Twitter feed. To say I was even half-interested in what my Uber driver was going to tell me would have been an exaggeration.

"A guy with a heart in his dick."

I looked up. Our eyes locked in the rearview mirror, and although I wanted to look away, I could not. "What do you mean?"

"I never seen a guy with a heart in his dick," he repeated in his New York City Dominican accent.

The ride was about to get weird. If I really wanted to, I could have stopped the conversation right there with a polite smile, nod, and look back down at my phone, and we would have continued the drive in silence. But what the fuck did he mean by a "heart in his dick?" Did he mean someone who fucks with passion? Or someone whose heart, the organ, was actually inside of his penis? I repeated my question, this time leaning forward, trying to crinkle my freshly Botoxed forehead.

He answered me again with his initial question. "You ever seen a guy with a heart in his dick?"

"I seriously don't know what you mean," I fake laughed. "I guess no, I haven't."

"I have a heart shape implanted in my dick," he said casually.

"Tell me everything," I replied.

It was something that always happened to me—getting overly friendly with the driver. Although, can I really say it was *happening to me* when I was such a willing participant? It usually started with them, saying something along the lines of "Where've I seen you before?" to which I would reply with the truth, that they had seen me sucking dick on the Internet. They'd have a million questions, and since porn is a subject I'm generally happy to talk about, before I knew it, I was ten minutes deep into a conversation I wished I hadn't started in the first place.

That day, I was taking an Uber cab from a meeting in midtown to my cousin's house in Brooklyn. We were still on the West Side Highway heading down to the bridge, and I knew that in this traffic, there was a good twenty minutes ahead of us. This meant I had twenty minutes to see my Uber driver's penis without giving the impression I was coming on to him.

"I can't believe you never seen one," he started. "I did it myself."

Instantly I was flooded with questions to ask, including the standard who, what, when, where, why, but I decided to start with "How?"

"I did it when I was in jail, all the guys do it."

This was getting even better.

"Hold on," I stopped him. "Why were you in jail?" For a moment I wondered if that was too personal of a question, but I quickly reminded myself that we were talking about his penis.

"It wasn't for nothing I actually did," he started. *It never is,* I thought. Everything I knew about criminals, I had learned on television.

"It was for stealin' cars, but I didn't do it. It's a long story. Anyway, so what you do is you take a domino—you know? Like the piece from the game?"

I nodded my head.

"You shave it down to a little ball, and you implant that in your dick. You gotta be careful though, 'cause if you get an infection, you get into trouble."

I laughed. "Wait, in jail they punish you for getting infections?"

"Nah," he shook his head at my naïvety. "Cause you not supposed to have tools and shit to shave a domino into a ball."

"Oh. But I thought you had a heart."

"Yeah, the first time I had a ball."

"How many times have you done it?"

"Every time I went to jail."

"How many times have you been to jail?" I laughed. I wondered if this was only funny to me. He didn't smile.

"Like, three times," he answered.

"Were you ever guilty?" I asked.

"No."

I had a feeling he would say that.

I sat quietly for a minute. Was this a conversation I really wanted to continue? This man was not only a criminal, but (at least) a three-time criminal. Yes, he claimed he was innocent, but that was probably a bad thing. What if he saw my interest as sexual? *Was* my interest sexual?

"So like, how do you do it?" I continued, ignoring my best judgment.

"You really wanna know?" he smiled. It should have creeped me out, but it didn't. "So you know where the extra skin is?"

"You mean the foreskin?" I asked, noting that a man who didn't know the word *foreskin* had earlier needed confirmation that I knew what a domino was.

"Yeah," he nodded.

I thought back to the Dominican guys I had fucked. Were they circumcised? I couldn't remember.

He continued, "So you know when you pull it back, you slice it right there. Then you lift the skin up and push the implant in."

"What if you don't have a foreskin?" I asked.

He shrugged.

"What do you slice it with?"

"That's the tricky part. Sometimes you can steal a razor. But sometimes you gotta do it with a piece of plastic you sharpened, and that's difficult."

I nodded in agreement—it did, in fact, sound difficult. "Do a lot of guys do it?"

"It's a Dominican thing," he answered. "Most guys do the ball one. They call it a 'pearl.' But I got a heart."

"Why did you change yours?"

"Most guys, you do a pearl for every year you're locked up."

"Wait, why?" I interrupted. I couldn't believe I hadn't asked this yet.

"Cause you in jail! What else are you gonna do?"

I thought of all of the things I would do in jail before implanting a domino piece in my genitals.

"So it's 'cause you're bored?"

"Nah," he laughed. "Well that too. But now when you get out, the girls love it," he smiled.

When he said that, I realized I couldn't believe I had never come across a man with this so-called pearl in his penis. I was from New York City. I had fucked numerous Dominicans. Surely, a couple of them had been in jail and were daring enough to cut their own dicks open?

"Ahh," I nodded. "I see. So it's to make sex better."

"Ex-aa-ctly. And when's a better time to do it? You ain't doing shit else anyway."

"Perr-fect," I matched his tone. "'Cause you're not fucking any girls anyway, you have plenty of time to heal." I saw the logic now. "But what about jerking off? Can you do that?"

He shook his head. "Nah, you can't touch it. Like I said, you get in trouble if you get an infection, 'cause then they know. It ain't worth it."

"That would be a really stupid way to get in trouble," I agreed. I remembered the time I had pierced my belly button in secret from my parents, and only when it got infected was the jig up.

We rode in silence as we each thought our own thoughts. I wondered if he was thinking I was going to hit on him. Or maybe he thought I already was. How was I going to see his dick? I'd have to climb into the front seat. The last time I sat up front in a cab, I ended up getting kicked out in the middle of nowhere at 4:00 a.m., scared out of my mind. I was a teen, and I had sat in the passenger seat so the driver and I could smoke a joint together. He had grabbed my pussy, and I froze. I vowed to always sit in the back seat from then on.

"So you said you had a heart now," I remembered aloud. "Why'd you change it?"

"'Cause when I was fucking girls and they saw it, they got weirded out."

I wondered which was weirder, a pearl or a heart. "Why were they weirded out?"

"I'd tell them what it was, and they didn't believe me."

"Oooh, like they thought it was a growth or a disease?" I pictured myself fucking a guy for the first time, pulling his dick out of his pants, and seeing a pearl-sized bump on his shaft. I had to agree, I would be suspicious.

"Yeah. So I made it a heart. It's cute, you know. Girls love it."

Unless it was in reference to a baby or a puppy, it turned me off when guys used the word "cute." That's not to say I was turned on at any point in this conversation—but if he had even had a slight chance before, it was completely gone now. Somehow, this was exactly what I had needed to ask to see it.

"Do you like have a picture of it or something?" I intentionally said this with a straight face so he wouldn't mistake it for flirting.

"Yeah, I got one on my phone. Just let me find it." He dug into his pockets.

"Isn't it right there?" I pointed to the iPhone on his dashboard.

"Nah, that's the Uber one. You can't take photos on it."

I was learning so much today.

Leaning back, I waited for him to find the photo on his phone. I was being a very irresponsible passenger—asking him to look in his phone while he was driving. I hoped this wouldn't affect my average customer rating. So far, I had 4.8 out of five stars. I wondered how many more Uber rides I would have to take with a five rating in order to achieve a 4.9 average. This was something I had given up on solving many times—I'm not the kind of Asian who is good at math.

"Here it is, it's not totally hard though," he apologized and passed the phone back to me.

There it was. A semi-hard uncircumcised penis with something vaguely shaped like a heart in the middle of the shaft. As much as I wanted to find it cute, as he had promised, I could not. I passed the phone back. "That's crazy!" I said in my best fake-enthused voice, and leaned back into my seat.

We drove the remaining few minutes in silence. I didn't know what more I could say now that I had seen his dick. He was probably thinking the same.

As I got out of the car, I opened up the Uber app on my phone to give him the five-star rating he deserved. On his profile, I saw that his name was Luis.

I hoped he gave me five stars too.

Haiku

Pimple on my cheek
Took five cum shots on my face
Pimple is gone now

SCRIPT

Written by

Asa Akira

FADE IN:

EXT. LAX AIRPORT—DAY

It's a typical sunny Los Angeles day at the airport. We see people walking around with their luggage, getting into cars, and standing in taxi lines.

                    ASA (V.O.)
          Los Angeles. Two thousand
          eight. It was the year my life
          changed. In a way, it was the

year I was born.

ASA (Asian female, twenty-three, wearing all black) comes through the doors with one duffel bag on her shoulder. She looks around, confused, as people around her get into cars.

                    ASA
              (to herself)
         Where is this guy...

After looking around some more, JENNA (ditzy blonde female, twenty-two, pretty but trashy; wearing a pink tanktop, short sweatshorts, and UGGs) comes walking toward Asa, arm waving.

                   JENNA
         Hey! Are you Ay-sa?

FREEZE FRAME on Jenna

                 ASA (V.O.)
         No one ever got my name right.
         But it was the name I grew up
         with, my real name, so I was
         used to it.

Jenna sticks out her hand to shake Asa's. Asa is at first confused, but relieved there is someone there to get her.

                    ASA
         It's Ah-suh. Yes! Nice to meet

you. Um...are you picking me
up?

> JENNA
> Oops, sorry. We weren't sure
> how to pronounce it. I'm
> Jenna. I'm Joel's girlfriend.
> They wouldn't let us park so
> he's circling the airport. He
> should be here soon.

The two girls walk over to a bench. Jenna sits
down. Asa stays standing, sets her bag on the
floor, and starts biting her nails.

> ASA
> So...what kind of car is he
> coming in?

> JENNA
> Joel drives an old-person car.
> It's so ugly. I can't. I just got
> a car. It's red. It's way cooler.

> ASA
> Cool...

Asa looks around, clearly feeling awkward. The
girls wait in silence.

Asa looks at Jenna, measuring her up and down.
Jenna is oblivious, completely engrossed in her
phone.

                    ASA (V.O.)
          She was everything you want a
          California girl to look like.
          The blonde hair.

ZOOM on Jenna tucking her hair behind her ear.

                    ASA (V.O.)
          The blue eyes.

ZOOM on Jenna's eyes quickly blinking, cellphone
glaring.

                    ASA (V.O.)
          The boobs. The shirt from
          Victoria's Secret, the sweat-
          shorts from Abercrombie and
          Fitch, the UGGs.

ZOOM on Jenna's breasts in her shirt. Then shorts.
Then UGGs.

                    ASA (V.O.)
          UGGs.

ZOOM even closer onto Jenna's UGGs.

Finally, after what seems like an eternity, JOEL
(White male, forties, used to be good-looking but is
now past his heyday, in khakis and a faded T-shirt)
drives up in what is, in fact, an old person's car: a
beige Lincoln. For the first time, we see Asa smile.
We can see she is happy to see him.

Joel gets out of the car.

CLOSEUP SHOT of Joel's small gold hoop earring.

CLOSEUP SHOT of the bleach stain on his shirt.

CLOSEUP SHOT of the hem of his pants, which are just above his ankles, revealing his slightly mismatched socks.

                    JOEL
              (enthusiastically)
          Hi! It's so nice to finally
          meet you in person! I'm Joel.
          Welcome to California!

                    ASA
          Nice to meet you, I'm Asa. I'm
          excited to be here.

Joel picks up the duffel bag.

                    JOEL
          Is this all you brought?

                    ASA
              (smiling)
          Yeah...I mean it's only one
          week?

                    JOEL
          Low maintenance, I like that.
          You should see what some of

the girls bring, it drives me
crazy what you girls consider
necessary.

INT. JOEL'S CAR—DAY

Joel is driving the car as Jenna sits up front
in the passenger seat, once again completely
engrossed in her phone. Asa sits in the backseat, looking out the window, taking in her first
impression of Los Angeles.

SHOTS OF PALM TREES

SHOTS OF OLD MEN WITH YOUNG GIRLS IN CONVERTIBLES

SHOT OF IN AND OUT

SHOT OF THE BACK OF JOEL'S HUGE HEAD. His hair is
messy and there are fuzz and crumbs in it.

> ASA (V.O.)
> Joel Lawrence. Ex-porn-star-
> turned-owner of the Goldstar
> Modeling Agency. He seemed
> nice enough on the phone.
> Plus, Gina had referred me to
> him. She said he was a nice
> guy. Who was I to dispute who
> in porn was a nice guy?

Joel is eating a sandwich as he drives.

GROTESQUE CLOSEUP SHOTS of him chewing his food.

                    JOEL
          (looking in the rearview)
          You look like your pictures.

Asa looks at Joel's face in the rearview mirror.

                    ASA
          Are you surprised?

                    JOEL
          You'd be shocked at what girls
          look like in person some-
          times. But you came with a
          high recommendation from Gina
          and Travis, so I felt pretty
          confident flying you out.

SHOT OF GINA LYNN AND TRAVIS KNIGHT WEDDING PHOTO

SHOT OF GINA LYNN AND TRAVIS KNIGHT MEETING ASA
AT A STRIP CLUB

SHOT OF ASA FUCKING GINA WHILE TRAVIS SHOOTS
CAMERA

SHOT OF ASA FUCKING TRAVIS WHILE GINA SHOOTS
CAMERA

                    ASA
          Thanks?

                         (pause)

              How long have you represented
              Gina for?

                              JOEL
              It's been a little over a
              year. She's great. So's Travis.
              I'm not sure if you know this,
              but Gina's, I'd say, one of
              the top three porn stars in
              the world right now. I repre-
              sent over a hundred girls, and
              she's my biggest star right
              now.

                              ASA
              Wow...

                              JOEL
              I have a feeling you'll be up
              there too.

        Jenna looks up from her phone and turns around.

                              JENNA
              You're an A-list girl.

                              ASA
              What do you mean?

                              JENNA
              It just means you're special.

                    ASA
Is there such a thing as a
B-list?

                    JOEL
Oh yeah. And a C-list. And a
D-list.

                    ASA
Do I even want to know what
that means?

                    JENNA
I'm a B-list.

               (to Joel)

What do you think, babe? Would
you say I'm B-list?

Joel places his hand on Jenna's lap sympatheti-
cally.

                    JOEL
You're still too new. We don't
know where you'll end up yet.

Asa sits up in her seat and leans closer to Jenna.

                    ASA
Wait, you're a porn star?

                    JENNA
                  (offended)
        Um, yeah. I don't have any
        makeup on right now, I...

                    ASA
        No! I didn't mean it like
        that. I'm sorry, I just don't
        know any...

                    JENNA
        It's fine.

Jenna looks out the window and crosses her arms.
Asa leans back in her seat. She starts to bite
her nails; she is looking at Jenna up and down
again.

CLOSEUP OF HAIR EXTENSIONS ON THE BACK OF JENNA'S
HEAD

CLOSEUP OF JENNA'S LONG FRENCH-TIP ACRYLIC NAILS

CLOSEUP OF JENNA'S LOUIS VUITTON PURSE

                    ASA (V.O.)
        Of course.

Asa sits back up and leans into Jenna.

                    ASA
        Wait, so how long have you
        been in the business?

                    JENNA
Three years.

                     ASA
And you're still considered
new?

                    JENNA
I didn't say that, Joel did.

                    JOEL
It's been really hard for poor
Jenna...

                    JENNA
I have psoriasis. The only
reason I came with Joel today
is 'cause I just had to cancel
an entire month of work. My
whole March was booked up!
That's like never happened.
And I had my first feature.
Now I won't even get to do
that.

                     ASA
What's a feature?

                    JENNA
It's a porno with dialogue.

                    JOEL
There's two kinds of porn:

features and gonzo. Features
are higher-budget productions
with story lines, and gonzos
are just all sex, no plot.

> ASA
> Which is better?

> JOEL
> That's not really how it works.
> Everyone does both. A feature
> set is more like shooting a
> mainstream movie. If you're a
> good actress, you get to do
> more features.

> JENNA
> Except me. I'll probably never
> get booked for a feature
> again.

Joel moves his hand up to Jenna's shoulder. It's
almost paternal.

> JOEL
> Aww sweetie. We'll figure it
> out.

The car pulls up into a driveway of an old house.
It's large but definitely needs some fixing up.

> JOEL
> Well, here we are. Welcome to Goldstar Modeling!

CLOSEUP on the overgrown lawn

CLOSEUP on the chipped paint on the house

CLOSEUP on the torn screen on the front door

Asa nervously smiles.

DISSOLVE TO:

INT. MODEL HOUSE/ASA'S BEDROOM—DAY
Joel and Asa stand in a small bedroom. It's not
dark, but not bright either. Not nice, but not
gross. Joel sets Asa's bag down on the bed.

> JOEL
> So this is your room. It's
> not much, but it's the nicest
> bedroom in the house. Aside
> from mine, of course.

Joel laughs at an extremely loud volume.
CAMERA ZOOM on his mouth as he laughs. Asa's
eyebrows raise.

> JOEL
> In a few hours, the makeup
> artist will be here, so you
> have some time to relax.

> ASA
> Makeup artist? For what?

> JOEL
> Oh, did I not tell you? You're
> shooting your agency photos
> today. There's gonna be some
> other girls coming to get
> theirs done too, so you'll get
> to meet them. In the meantime,
> Jenna and I are going to the
> grocery store...do you want
> anything specific?

> ASA
> Um...some fruit would be
> great.

> JOEL
> You got it. Holler if you need
> anything.

Joel leaves the room, shutting the door behind him. Asa sits down on the bed and looks around the room.

CLOSEUP OF STAIN ON CARPET

CLOSEUP OF RANDOM EARRING-BACK ON THE NIGHTSTAND

She looks at her phone. It reads *ONE UNREAD MESSAGE*. She opens it up, and we see that it is from EVAN (cut here to a shot over her shoulder). *You get there okay?* She writes back, *Yeah. Every-thing good. Don't worry.* He replies immediately, with a frowny face emoji.

                    ASA (V.O.)
        I couldn't make him happy,
        while making myself happy too.
        It was me or him. I chose me.
        I just hope I made the right
        decision.

FAST MONTAGE OF HAPPY TIMES WITH EVAN:

Meeting for the first time > fucking on top of
Ralph Lauren teddy-bear sheets > yelling at each
other > throwing things > crying as they part
ways at the airport.

Asa lies down to take a nap.

DISSOLVE TO:

INT. MODEL HOUSE/ASA'S BEDROOM—DAY, COUPLE HOURS
LATER

It's a few hours later, and Asa is waking up
from her nap. Everything is in exactly the same
place, including the duffel bag at the edge of the
bed. We hear lots of people talking and laughing
outside of the room, mostly female voices.

Asa slowly gets up and walks toward the door.

INT. MODEL HOUSE/LIVING ROOM—CONTINUING

Asa comes out of her room to find half a dozen
girls in various states of undress walking around
the house. Everyone is talking loudly. LILLY
(flashy Latina female, late thirtiess) the makeup
artist is working on RENEE (brunette female, like
thirty-ish).

Lilly notices Asa.

> LILLY
> There she is! You're up! Come
> here.

Lilly turns to Renee.

> LILLY
> Sorry baby, Joel told me to
> get her in as soon as she woke
> up. I'll finish you once I'm
> done with her.

Renee rolls her eyes and drags herself out of the
chair. She doesn't acknowledge Asa.

> LILLY
> Come, come, sit. I've been
> looking forward to meeting
> you! Everyone's been really
> excited.

> ASA
> Thank you. I'm excited to be
> here.

                    LILLY
          I'm Lilly, your makeup artist.
          So they want something kind of
          a smoky brown natural, is that
          okay?

FREEZE FRAME on Lilly.

                    ASA (V.O.)
          Smoky what?

Asa shrugs.

Lilly gets to work.

Asa looks around the room. By the kitchen, ABBY
and KATY (two young porn girls) are talking.

                    ABBY
          I was like, are you fucking
          kidding me? Don't blame your
          soft dick on me. This has
          nothing to do with me. This
          has to do with you being gay.

                    KATY
          Girl I've heard so many
          stories like that about him.
          He's on my NO list.

                    ABBY
          You're smart. I just kept
          thinking...motherfucker, I

would *never* fuck you if I
weren't getting paid. Fucking
NEVER.

SLOWLY PAN OVER TO THE SOFA.

KATRINA (blonde porn girl in lingerie) is on the phone.

                    KATRINA
                  (on phone)
No baby, it's just fucking
photos.

Well I need new photos for the
website! The ones on there now
don't even look like me—I'm
still a brunette and I have
three more tattoos now!

What the fuck do you want
me to do now? Leave? I'm not
doing that.

There aren't any guys here.

Why would I lie about that??

IT'S JUST PHOTOS! THERE AREN'T
EVEN ANY GUYS HERE!

I'M NOT YELLING!

                  (pause)

You're just driving me nuts.

SLOWLY PAN OVER TO DOORWAY TO BACKYARD.

BELLA, MANDY, and SARA (porn girls) are smoking.

                    MANDY
          I'm from Florida too! What
          part are you from?

                    BELLA
          Miami. You?

                    MANDY
          Fort Lauderdale.

                    BELLA
          That's so crazy! Have you shot
          anything there?

                    MANDY
          Ugh. Yes. It's so different.

                    BELLA
          I know. I hated it.

                    SARA
          I shot there too. It's a
          different world. I'm only doing
          LA shoots now.

                    BELLA
          Did you do that dorm room one?

                    SARA
Yes! Oh my god it was
terrible!

                   MANDY
Oh my god, I heard that guy is
a total creep.

                    SARA
He roofied my friend and she's
all fucked up about it now.
He's bad news.

                   BELLA
The same thing happened to MY
friend!

                   MANDY
I'm so glad I'm here now...

SLOWLY PAN OVER BACK TO WHERE ASA IS SITTING. We
see Renee. She is sitting with her arms crossed,
staring, no, GLARING right at Asa.

                   RENEE
So, you think you're hot shit?

Asa looks up at Renee, then looks around to see
who she's talking to. Lilly forces her face back
to the front.

LILLY
Oh don't move baby, I'm doing
your eyes.

ASA
Sorry, I wasn't sure who she
was...

RENEE
Yeah, I was talking to you. So
you think you're hot shit?

Asa looks over at Renee again.

ASA
I'm sorry, what?

Lilly forces Asa's face back to the front again.

LILLY
Okay I *really* need you to you
stay facing me, I still have
three girls to do after you and
if you keep turning that way,
we'll never get out of here.

ASA
(facing Lilly this time)
What did she say to me?

RENEE
I *said*, do. You. Think. You.
Are. Hot. Shit.

                    ASA
                 No...why?

                   RENEE
            Everyone at the office has
            been talking about you. And
            now apparently your makeup
            is more important than mine.
            I've been in the business
            for eleven years, I've seen
            hundreds of girls like you
            come and go.

                    ASA
            I'm sorry, I didn't mean...

                   LILLY
            Renee, why don't you go some-
            where else so I can finish her
            up?

Renee stands up and walks toward Lilly and Asa.

Just then, Joel and Jenna walk in the door, arm
in arm, laughing. Joel immediately sees what's
going on.

                   JOEL
            Hey ladies, what's going on
            here?

Everyone in the room stops their conversation
and looks over at Renee.

                    RENEE
Why the fuck did Lilly just
kick me out of the chair for
the new girl?

                    JOEL
Okay, first of all, calm
down...

                    RENEE
I am calm!

Renee pouts and sits back down.

                    JOEL
Asa doesn't have photos up yet.
Renee, you already have a set up.

                    RENEE
I'm so sick of this shit. I've
been in this business for over
ten fucking years. Who the
fuck is she? Why the fuck is
she getting special treatment?

                    JOEL
She's not getting special
treatment, Renee. We talked
about this. Why don't you go
cool off?

                    RENEE
I'm so sick of seeing these

> new bitches get treated like
> gold while you treat me like a
> piece of shit. I could go over
> to LA Direct in a second, you
> know. They'd probably get me
> more work.

>   JOEL
> Come on Renee, don't be like
> that. Just relax, you...

>   RENEE
> Don't tell me to fucking relax,
> Joel! You know what...

Renee gets back up, and starts grabbing her things.

>   RENEE
> I'm fucking done with you.

Renee gets all her things and leaves, as Joel shakes his head. She slams the door behind her. Everyone is silent for a second before they go back to their own conversations.

>   ASA
> I'm sorry, I don't know what
> happened.

>   JOEL
> Don't be sorry, Renee is one

of our crazy ones. She's a
pain in the ass.

                    ASA
Well it looks like you won't
have to deal with her anymore.

                    JOEL
Oh, no. She'll be back. She's
like a cockroach.

Jenna walks over to Asa.

                    JENNA
We got you fruit. Don't worry
about Renee, no one likes her.
She's crazy. Her boyfriend
beats her.

                    ASA
Hmm.

DISSOLVE TO:

MONTAGE OF ASA'S FIRST WEEK IN PORN.

                    ASA (V.O.)
That first week was a blur.
I got through the photoshoot
without pissing anyone else
off.

SHOTS OF PHOTOSHOOT

>   ASA (V.O.)
>   I met with Vince Vouyer,
>   owner of Vouyer Media, and he
>   gave me a six-month exclusive
>   contract on the spot.

SHOTS OF VINCE LOOKING ASA UP AND DOWN FROM
BEHIND HIS DESK.

SHOTS OF VINCE/ASA SHAKING HANDS, THEN VINCE/JOEL
SHAKING HANDS.

>   ASA (V.O.)
>   I didn't meet many other
>   girls, but I did see a lot of
>   Jenna. Between her psoriasis
>   and me waiting an entire two
>   weeks to do my first shoot for
>   Vince, we had a lot of time to
>   get acquainted.

SHOTS OF JENNA AND ASA SHOPPING FOR LINGERIE,
LAUGHING, BONDING.

DISSOLVE TO:

EXT. MODEL HOUSE/POOL—DAY
Jenna and Asa are out by the pool. The mood is
very serene; there is no one else around. Asa is
lying on her stomach, texting on her phone; Jenna

is sitting at the edge of the pool dangling her
feet in the water.

>   JENNA
>   Who are you always texting
>   with?

>   ASA
>   My ex-boyfriend.

>   JENNA
>   Are you trying to get back
>   with him?

>   ASA
>   I don't know. He hates that
>   I'm here.

>   JENNA
>   I had a boyfriend like that
>   when I got in too.

>   ASA
>   How long have you been with
>   Joel?

>   JENNA
>   Since Valentine's Day. So, a
>   month.

>   ASA
>   Oh, so it's a new thing?

                    JENNA
          Yeah.

                     ASA
          So you're still in the
          exciting part.

                    JENNA
          Not really. I kind of hate
          him.

                     ASA
          Wait, why are you with him
          then?

                    JENNA
          I mean...I'm just gonna wait
          until I figure out how to
          manage my psoriasis. I'm not
          doing anything right now
          anyway. With Joel I have a
          place to live, I don't have
          to pay for anything...plus he
          keeps me from being a crack-
          head.

                     ASA
          You mean, literally?

                    JENNA
          Sort of. Well, I was on meth.

FREEZE FRAME

> ASA (V.O.)
> I had never met anyone on
> meth. Back in New York, meth
> was just a myth; I read an
> article about it once in
> *Rolling Stone* magazine, where
> this entire farming town
> was on it and let all their
> animals and crops die. The
> recovery rate was a mere four
> percent, and the children of
> the town were unable to count
> to ten.

Asa sits up.

> ASA
> But...your face...it isn't a
> *methface*.

> JENNA
> I get that a lot. I dunno how,
> I was on it for three years.

> ASA
> You seem so put together.

> JENNA
> I'm not.

> ASA
> Well for someone who did
> meth...

                    JENNA
          Everyone does meth.

                    ASA
          Not in New York.

                    JENNA
          Welcome to California.

Jenna gets up and starts walking around the edge
of the pool, like on a balance beam. Asa goes
back to lying on her stomach. The girls go back
to silence for a while.

                    ASA
          So...why do you hate Joel?

                    JENNA
          I shouldn't have said that to
          you. He's a good agent. Don't
          worry.

                    ASA
          ...But he's a bad boyfriend?

                    JENNA
          No. He's just...gross. You've
          seen him eat. And the way he
          laughs...

                    ASA
          What IS that? I've never heard
          anyone laugh like that.

JENNA
And he only does it at his own
jokes. He's just really old
and gross. I'm not sexually
attracted to him. Thank god I
hardly have to see him.

Jenna's phone rings. She runs over to pick it up.
Asa goes back to texting.

SHOT OVER JENNA'S SHOULDER. We see the call is
from JAVIER. Jenna picks up.

JENNA
(on phone)
Hey Javi!

Nothing. I'm lying outside with
the new girl.

Yeah. That one.

Okay I'll ask her. I'll call
you back.

Jenna hangs up the phone.

JENNA
Wanna go to a pool party?

ZOOM SUPER CLOSE INTO JENNA'S DEVIOUS SMILE UNTIL
BLACK SCREEN.

EXT. MANSION/POOL—DAY

ZOOM OUT FROM JENNA'S MOUTH TO REVEAL WIDE SHOT
OF POOL PARTY AT ENORMOUS MANSION. Decor can only
be described as gaudy. There are people everywhere; it's pretty crowded and loud. Jenna is on
the phone looking for Javier.

                    JENNA
                 (on phone)
           Where? I don't see you? We're
           by the catering.

Jenna holds her arm up and waves. Just then,
JAVIER (tall Latino male, very good-looking, in
super good shape, late twenties) shows up, also
holding his arm up, with his friend ROMAN (shorter,
European male, also in very good shape, also late
twenties). Asa is looking around in awe.

                    JAVIER
                 (with accent)
           Hey baby, there you are! Sexy
           mami!

Javier picks Jenna up and she squeals. He puts
her down, and she gives Roman a hug.

                    Javier
           And this must be the new
           girl...

Javier wraps his hands around Asa's waist. She is taken aback, but doesn't push him away.

> ASA
> (laughing nervously)
> Nice to meet you. I'm Asa.

Everyone does the friendly introduction thing.

WIDE SHOT, we catch Javier asking if Asa wants a drink. Asa declines and Javier gives her a disappointed look. But he quickly recovers.

> JAVIER
> Okay then. Let's party!

MUSIC TURNS UP AND WE SEE A MONTAGE OF PARTYING. SHOTS OF DANCING, EATING, MEETING NEW PEOPLE, SWIMMING. (At one point, Roman tries to make out with Asa, but she laughingly pushes him away.) LAND ON SHOT of Asa lying by the pool. Jenna is in the background talking to Javier.

> ASA (V.O.)
> A real Hollywood party. It was exactly as I had seen in the movies. Everyone was either beautiful or rich. Even a Corey Feldman lookalike was there.

SHOT OF COREY FELDMAN LOOKALIKE ON A FLOAT IN
THE POOL. Corey Feldman Lookalike looks up and
sees Asa. He whispers something to the girl on
the float with him. They start to paddle over.

> ASA (V.O.)
> Shit. Was Corey Feldman Looka-
> like coming toward me?

JUMP CUTS OF COREY FELDMAN LOOKALIKE COMING
CLOSER, AND THEN CLOSER, AND THEN CLOSER. He
looks very high/drunk and very uncoordinated.

> ASA (V.O.)
> Yes. Corey Feldman Lookalike
> was coming toward me.

Corey Feldman Lookalike arrives in front of Asa.

> COREY FELDMAN LOOKALIKE
> Hi, I'm Corey Feldman.

FREEZE FRAME ON COREY FELDMAN.

> ASA (V.O.)
> Oh. It's actually Corey Feldman.

UNFREEZE. Everyone around continues talking.

> ASA
> Hi, I'm Asa.

> COREY
> This is my girlfriend.

            COREY'S GIRLFRIEND
                (slurring)
        Are you enjoying the party?

                    ASA
        I am. You?

            COREY'S GIRLFRIEND
        Oh yeah.

                    COREY
        We come here at least once a
        month.

                    ASA
        To this house?

                    COREY
        Yeah. I've never seen you
        here.
                    ASA
        I've never been here. I just
        got to LA last week.

                    COREY
        Where you from?

                    ASA
        New York City.

                    COREY
        I love it there. Are you an
        actress?

                        ASA
                     (smiling)
              Something like that.

                        COREY
              Ohhh, I know what that means.
              We have a lot of people in
              porn here.

Asa laughs, a little bashfully.

                        COREY
              So, do you know Yuval?

                        ASA
              Yuval Sherman?

                        COREY
              Who's Yuval Sherman?

                        ASA
              A kid I went to elementary
              school with. He's the only
              Yuval I know, and you asked if
              I knew Yuval.

                        COREY
              No, I mean Yuval Gold, the guy
              who owns this house.

Corey's Girlfriend is nodding off on the float.
Corey pays no mind to this.

ASA
No, I don't know anyone. I
came here with a girlfriend.

COREY
Oh, who's your girlfriend?

ASA
Jenna. She's...

Asa looks behind her in search of Jenna. She
finds her right there, making out with Javier. She
points to her.

ASA
She's right there. The one
making out with the guy.

COREY
She's cute.
            (pause)
But not as cute as you.

FREEZE FRAME ON COREY.

ASA (V.O.)
Was Corey Feldman hitting on
me?

UNFREEZE FRAME

COREY
I really love Asian girls.

FREEZE FRAME AGAIN ON COREY

> ASA (V.O.)
> Oh god. Corey Feldman was
> hitting on me. (pause) Is this
> cool? Or euw?

UNFREEZE FRAME

> COREY
> Like I said, we come here
> at least once a month...but
> it's been a while since we've
> played with an Asian girl.

Asa looks up and about. PAN OVER PARTY. EVERYONE
IS MAKING OUT, IT'S NOT JUST JENNA. PEOPLE ARE
FUCKING EVERYWHERE.

Asa walks over to Jenna and pulls her away from
Javier, apologizing to him.

> JENNA
> Ow, what the fuck?

> ASA
> Why didn't you tell me this
> was (whispering) a *swinger
> party*?

> JENNA
> It is?

                    ASA
          Yeah, look around!

Jenna laughs, putting her arm around Asa.

                   JENNA
          Welcome to LA, baby...

                    ASA
          Whatever. This is really
          uncomfortable. I'm calling
          a cab. You can stay or come
          with.

Asa turns around and walks away as Jenna laughs
and waves.

CUT TO:

INT. MANSION/HALLWAY—CONTINUING

Asa walks by people in various states of sex. She
knocks on the bathroom door, but there are people
inside fucking. She goes to a somewhat quieter
corner and calls a cab.

CUT TO:

INT. TAXI—DAY

Asa's cellphone vibrates. SHOT OVER HER SHOULDER.

We see that it's a message from Evan: *When are you coming home?* She replies: *I dunno.* He replies: *Are you still sure about this?* She looks out the window, thinking. She replies: *I dunno.*

DISSOLVE TO:

INT. SHOOT HOUSE/LIVING ROOM—DAY

Asa, in sweats and a hoodie, is getting her makeup done once again by Lilly. The shoot house they are in is another gaudy mansion, much like the one from the pool party. VINCE (stocky man in his forties, good-looking, in good shape, has an HGH vibe) is standing by her, talking to her as THE PA (young Mexican guy, looks slightly convict-ish) is moving lights and furniture.

> VINCE
> Have you ever been with two
> guys before?

> ASA
> Once.

> VINCE
> How'd you like it?

> ASA
> (smiling)
> I loved it.

CUT TO:

INT. SHOOT HOUSE/LIVING ROOM—CONTINUING

Asa, now in lingerie, is posing for photos on a white seamless background as Lilly periodically steps in to fix her hair.

                    VINCE
          Are you nervous?

                    ASA
          I'm not sure. I think I'm more
          excited, than anything. They
          have really big dicks. I hope
          I can take them.

                    VINCE
          I think you'll be fine. If you
          can't, we can just cut, and
          we'll find a replacement. It's
          not a big deal.

                    ASA
          Has that ever happened before?

Vince thinks about it for a moment.

                    VINCE
          Not to my knowledge.

                    ASA
          Oh my god, I really do not

want to be the first one to do
that. Okay, actually I think I
am nervous.

                  VINCE
I saw what you did with
Travis, and you were good. I
don't think you're gonna have
any problems.

                  ASA
I dunno...I mean that felt
really different than this.
It was way more casual. And
I knew him beforehand. And I
mean, his dick wasn't as big
as these guys'.

                  VINCE
Yeah, but you love fucking. I
can tell you love performing.
Trust me. I really think
you're gonna be fine.

Asa looks nervous as she continues posing for
photos.

CUT TO:

INT. SHOOT HOUSE/LIVING ROOM—CONTINUING

Vince stands behind the cameraman, talking with him about camera stuff, as Asa sits between TWO MALE PERFORMERS, JERRY and SASCHA (both buff, both good-looking).

                    JERRY
          So, Vince says this is your
          first scene?

                    ASA
          Sort of, yeah. It's my first
          scene in LA. I did a bunch
          of girl-girl stuff with Gina
          Lynn, and I've only done one
          boy-girl scene...it was with
          her husband. At their house in
          Pennsylvania. It felt really
          different than this.

                    SASCHA
          Different how?

                    ASA
Well I mean, like, it was just less people
around, and the whole thing felt way more
amateur...

                    SASCHA
          Did you have fun? Like, did
          you like it?

> ASA
> Oh, I definitely did.

> SASCHA
> Then there's nothing to be
> worried about. The sets
> change, but if you like doing
> porn, then you like doing
> porn.

Asa smiles, then they sit in awkward silence.

> VINCE
> Okay then, we're ready to
> roll. Does anyone need
> anything before we start?

Everyone shakes their heads.

> VINCE
> Alright, let's start with Asa
> fucking you first

Vince points to Jerry.

> VINCE
> Right here on the sofa, and
> then after a while, we'll move
> to the bathroom, and all three
> of you can continue fucking in
> there.

Everyone nods their heads, and Sascha gets up.

> VINCE
> Okay, let's start with you
> guys kissing, and just let it
> go from there.
>
> Aaaand "ACTION."

Jerry and Asa start kissing. It's very awkward. Very rigid.

SHOT OF PA COUGHING

SHOT OF SOUND GUY ADJUSTING HIS MACHINERY

SHOT OF VINCE PURSING HIS LIPS

But then Jerry puts his hand on Asa's pussy, and slowly, we see her start to melt. She moans, and everything starts to look much more relaxed. He makes her orgasm—and then, it's on.

FAST-PACED MONTAGE OF THE SEX SCENE. "YOUR FUCKIN HEAD SPLIT" BY NECRO PLAYS. SHOTS OF ASA GETTING FUCKED IN DIFFERENT POSITIONS. WE CAN TELL ASA IS HAVING THE TIME OF HER LIFE. ARTISTIC CUMSHOT ALL OVER HER FACE. MONTAGE ENDS WITH ASA IN THE SHOWER, SMILING.

Asa, wrapped in a towel and with wet hair, comes out of the shower and back into the living room where Jerry and Sascha are sitting on the sofa doing their paperwork, the cameraman, PA, and

sound guy are packing up the equipment, and Vince
is leaning against the pool table.

> VINCE
> Whadju think, boys?

> JERRY
> She's fucking good. I'm worn out.

> SASCHA
> (to Asa)
> You're going to be a very,
> very big star.

> VINCE
> Good. Asa, you looked like you
> were enjoying yourself.

Asa goes to lie on the sofa and takes out her
phone from her purse. One of the male talents
grabs her foot and starts massaging it.

> ASA
> That...was fucking amazing. I
> can't believe this is my life.

Her phone vibrates. SHOT OVER HER SHOULDER. *One
unread message*. It's from Evan. *Are you absolutely sure?*

Asa smiles.
She replies: *Yes.*

Haiku

Unfertilized eggs
Go ahead, bleed down my leg
I'm not done whoring

Acknowledgments

Thank you, first and foremost, to Karen Thomas and everyone at Cleis Press for publishing *Dirty Thirty*.

Thank you to my literary suitcase pimp, Marc Gerald.

Thank you to my actual pimp, Mark Spiegler.

Thank you to Wicked Pictures for keeping me under contract and producing top notch smut.

Thank you to my parents for creating me in that test tube and then growing me in a small petri dish before later transferring me to a larger petri dish and finally birthing me in literally any way but through mom's vagina.

Thank you to the best artist in the world, David Choe, for the beautiful cover art.

Thank you "Dee."

Thank you to everyone who is in this book, I love you all. (Except for those I talked shit about, whose names are changed anyway.)

Thank you to the reader. If you don't want to jerk off to my porn anymore, I understand.